Grand Diplôme® Cooking Course

Volume 17

Grand Diplôme® Cooking Course

A Danbury Press Book

The Danbury Press

a division of Grolier Enterprises, Inc.

Robert B. Clarke   Publisher

This book has been adapted from the Grand Diplôme Cooking Course, originally published by Purnell Cookery, U.S.A.

Purnell Grand Diplôme Editorial Board

Rosemary Hume and Muriel Downes
Principals, London Cordon Bleu Cookery
School, England

Anne Willan	Editor
Eleanor Noderer	Associate Editor
Sheryl Julian	Assistant Editor
John Paton	Managing Editor
José Northey	Co-ordinating Editor
Peter Leather	Art Editor
Charles F. Turgeon	Wine Consultant
Joy Langridge	Consultant Editor

Library of Congress Catalog Card Number: 72-13896
© Phoebus Publishing Company/BPC Publishing Limited, 1971/1972/1979
Filmsetting by Petty and Sons Ltd., Leeds, England.
Printed in the United States of America

4567899

All recipes have been tested either at the Cordon Bleu Cookery School in London or in our U.S. test kitchens.

Note: all recipe quantities in this book serve 4 people unless otherwise stated.

Contents

Game is a gourmet's delight — pheasant Vallée d'Auge in a sauce with apples and cream; partridges baked with black olives and wine; venison steaks spiced with juniper berries — you'll find all these dishes and many more in Volume 17 of your Grand Diplôme Cooking Course.

When game is out of season, turn to some eye-catching **Classic Entrées** of beef, lamb, veal and chicken suggested by the Cordon Bleu Cookery School in London. Dishes like lamb chops Alsacienne covered with ham and pâté and simmered in sherry or Hungarian grenadins of veal, gently browned with eggplant slices and a mornay sauce, are specially designed to be easy to serve. Garnish and meat are arranged on one platter, so no accompaniment is necessary.

The cooking of Canton has inspired innumerable westerners to tackle the oriental intricacies of **Chinese Cooking**. Consider the subtle combinations of the eight basic flavors — salty, bland, sweet, sour, bitter, hot, fragrant and golden. Progress from simple stir-fried Chinese chard (yow yim bok choy) to banquet specialties like lotus stuffed duck (leen gee opp) and winter melon soup (doong gwa joong). You'll find more delicious ideas for duck in **Chicken and Duck Dishes** — try succulent roast duck with caramelized fresh peaches or a cold stuffed duck with tart lemon compote. Give a chicken an eastern flavor by combining it with mango slices or prepare it Persian style with tomatoes, almonds and raisins.

Greet your guests appropriately with one of our luncheon **Menus** planned to suit the season — chicken is garnished with green grapes for spring, salmon shimmers in aspic for summer, crêpes are stuffed for the fall and beef is sautéed with mushrooms and wine for a warming winter entrée. For formal occasions, you have a choice of three superb menus, each one featuring classic recipes of French cuisine. So tie your aprons, don your toques blanches and Bon Appétit!

Anne Willan

Apple and hazelnut galette, topped with rosettes of whipped cream, makes a delicious dessert for spring (the recipe is on page 12)

CHOOSE LUNCHEON MENUS TO FIT THE SEASON

Take your choice of our menus to suit each season of the year. Greet the spring with refreshing chicken Véronique garnished with green grapes; celebrate summer with salmon in sparkling aspic; enjoy autumn with savory crêpes, and welcome the winter with a hearty sauté of beef with mushrooms. All menus are planned to avoid last-minute preparation, and each serves 12 people.

With chicken Véronique, try a Traminer from Alsace or California. The salmon would be complemented by a Sancerre from France's Loire valley or a California Chenin Blanc. A dry, white Graves from Bordeaux or a dry Semillon from California would suit the chicken crêpes. With the sauté of beef, try a Gigondas from France's Côte du Rhône or perhaps a California Zinfandel.

Spring Menu

Appetizer

Seafood and Watercress Cocktail

For fish mousse
2 lb fresh haddock fillet
1 cup thick white sauce (made
  with 3 tablespoons butter,
  3 tablespoons flour and
  1 cup milk)
salt and pepper
juice of 1 lemon
2 packages (3 oz each) cream
  cheese
2 tablespoons chopped chives
$\frac{1}{4}$ cup finely chopped
  watercress stems
about 6 tablespoons heavy
  cream

For shrimp mixture
1 lb cooked, peeled medium
  shrimps
1 teaspoon paprika
2 tablespoons ketchup
$2\frac{1}{2}$ cups mayonnaise
$\frac{1}{2}$ cup chopped celery
1 tablespoon prepared
  horseradish

Method

Set oven at moderate (350°F).

To prepare fish mousse: make white sauce and chill it. Place haddock in a buttered baking dish, season and squeeze over lemon juice. Cover with buttered foil and bake in heated oven for about 15 minutes or until fish flakes easily when tested with a fork. Let stand until cool. Flake the fish, removing any skin and bones, and crush flesh with a fork. Beat in the cold white sauce and cream cheese. When mixture is quite smooth, stir in chives and watercress stems.

Watchpoint: the watercress stems must be stripped of all leaves and very finely chopped. There should be enough to give the mousse an attractive green color and a peppery flavor – adjust the amount to your taste.

Stir in enough heavy cream so the mixture will drop from a spoon and season to taste.

To prepare shrimp mixture: mix paprika and ketchup with the mayonnaise. Season to taste and add chopped celery and horseradish. Fold in the shrimps and arrange alternate layers of the fish mousse and the shrimp mixture in stemmed wine or sundae glasses, starting and finishing with the shrimp mixture.

Alternative appetizer

Consommé with Caviar

7 cans beef consommé
1 envelope gelatin
1 tablespoon tomato paste
  (optional)
6 tablespoons sherry
  (optional)
black pepper, freshly ground

For serving
1 small jar of red caviar
$\frac{1}{2}$ cup sour cream
12 lemon wedges

Method

Sprinkle the gelatin over 1 can consommé and let stand 5 minutes until spongy; dissolve over low heat. If adding tomato paste, mix it with a little of the remaining consommé before adding it to the rest. Pour the consommé into a pitcher and stir in the dissolved gelatin and sherry, if using. Add a little freshly ground pepper, stir well and chill the consommé overnight; it will be fairly firmly set.

Stir the consommé to break it up slightly and spoon it into chilled soup cups. Top each cup with 2 teaspoons of sour cream and a teaspoon of caviar and place a wedge of lemon at the side. Cover and keep the cups chilled until serving.

TIMETABLE

Day before
Cook haddock; store covered in refrigerator. Make sauce for shrimps, cover and refrigerate, *or add gelatin, sherry and tomato paste to consommé and chill.*

Cook chickens and carve them; make sauce but do not add grapes, spoon over chicken and leave in sauce ready for reheating. Make potato cakes, leave in pans ready for reheating.

Wash greens for salad and keep in plastic bag in refrigerator; make vinaigrette dressing.

Make and bake hazelnut pastry rounds and store in an airtight container. Make filling, cover and refrigerate.

Morning
Complete seafood cocktails, cover and chill, *or lightly stir consommé, spoon into cups, garnish and chill.*

Complete and decorate galette.

Just before serving
Reheat chicken and julienne potato cakes in a moderate oven (350°F) for 20–25 minutes or until very hot.

Drain and arrange chicken with potato cakes on platters, add grapes to sauce, reheat and spoon over chicken.

Toss salad with vinaigrette dressing.

All recipes in these seasonal menus serve 12 people, so remember to triple the quantities of any recipes you use from another Volume.

Entrée

Chicken Véronique

3 roasting chickens
(3–3½ lb each)
salt and pepper
¾ cup butter
6–8 sprigs of fresh tarragon
or 1 tablespoon dried
tarragon
1 lb seedless green grapes
juice of ½ lemon
4 cups chicken stock
1 tablespoon arrowroot
(mixed to a paste with
¼ cup water)
¾ cup heavy cream
pinch of sugar

Trussing needle and string

Method

Set oven at hot (400°F).

Wipe inside the birds with a damp cloth, sprinkle inside with seasoning, add 1 tablespoon butter and tarragon and truss them. Spread remaining butter over the birds, set them in a large roasting pan, cover loosely with buttered foil and roast in heated oven for 1 hour or until the juice runs clear when birds are pierced in the thigh with a skewer. Baste and turn from time to time.

Take grapes from the stems, add lemon juice and cover.

Remove birds from oven when cooked and keep hot. Discard excess fat from roasting pan and reduce pan juices, if necessary, by boiling until they are brown and sticky. Add stock and bring to a boil, stirring, to deglaze pan. Simmer 1–2 minutes, strain into a saucepan, bring to a boil and thicken slightly by whisking in the arrowroot paste. Add the cream, bring back just

to a boil and keep warm.

Cut up the birds into 5 pieces each and arrange on 2 large platters around or on top of the julienne potato cakes. Add grapes and their liquid to sauce, reheat well, taste for seasoning, adding sugar, and spoon a little sauce over the birds. Serve the remaining sauce separately. A green salad makes a good accompaniment.

Arrange the chicken Véronique on top of the julienne potato cake. Pour over a little sauce, with the grapes, and serve the rest separately with a fresh green salad

Dessert

Apple and Hazelnut Galette

2¾ cups hazelnuts, browned
1¼ cups butter
¾ cup sugar
3 cups flour
½ teaspoon salt
2–3 tablespoons water
  (optional)

For filling
10 Delicious or other firm
  dessert apples, pared, cored
  and sliced
¼ cup apricot jam
grated rind of 3 lemons
peeled rind of 2 oranges, finely
  chopped
½ cup raisins
½ cup currants or golden
  raisins

To decorate
confectioners' sugar
  (for sprinkling)
1 cup heavy cream, stiffly
  whipped (optional)

Method
Reserve ¼ cup whole hazelnuts for decoration; work remaining nuts through a rotary grater or work them, a few at a time, in a blender until they are finely ground.

To make galette: cream butter, beat in sugar gradually until light and soft. Sift flour with salt and stir into creamed mixture with ground nuts. Work to a smooth dough, adding a little water if necessary to hold it together. Wrap in wax paper; chill 30 minutes or until firm.

Set the oven at moderately hot (375°F); lightly flour 2 baking sheets.

To make filling: put apple slices in a pan with apricot jam and lemon rind. Cover

and cook over low heat for 10–15 minutes or until soft. Add orange rind, dried fruit and simmer mixture for about 5 minutes longer.

Divide dough in four and put 1 piece on each prepared baking sheet. Roll or pat out into very thin 10 inch rounds. Bake in heated oven for about 10 minutes or until just beginning to brown around edges. Repeat with remaining dough. **Watchpoint**: do not let pastry brown too much or it will taste scorched.

While rounds are still warm on baking sheets, trim edges, neatly cut 2 circles into 6–8 wedges, carefully transfer to a wire rack and cool. When uncut circles are cold, spread apple mixture over them and place wedges on top. Sprinkle with confectioners' sugar. If you like, decorate galette with rosettes of whipped cream and hazelnuts.

TIMETABLE

Day before
Cook salmon and cool. Make aspic. Set salmon on platter and add shrimps and aspic coating now (or in morning, if preferred); cover and keep in refrigerator.
Make mayonnaise Nantua.
Make vinaigrette dressing for cucumber salad.
Make and freeze pecan parfait.

Morning
Make soup and chill.
Add shrimps and aspic coating to salmon (if not done before). Garnish with cucumber and watercress. Finish cucumber salad and chill. Peel and slice peaches and leave to macerate.

Just before serving
Add garnish to soup.
Top parfait with peaches and decorate if you like.

Summer Menu

Iced Shannon Soup

*Salmon in Aspic
Mayonnaise Nantua*

Cucumber Salad

*Pecan Parfait
with Peaches*

*White wine – Sancerre (Loire)
or Chenin Blanc (California)*

Appetizer

Iced Shannon Soup

3 cans beef consommé
1 can (11 oz) vegetable juice
  cocktail
1 can (11 oz) tomato juice
dash of Tabasco
½ cup heavy cream

For serving
2 lemons, cut in wedges
½ cup heavy cream, whipped
  until it holds a soft shape
  (optional)
½ teaspoon grated nutmeg
  (optional)

Method
In a large bowl combine the consommé, vegetable and tomato juices and Tabasco and whisk together thoroughly. Stir in the cream and pour into soup bowls. Chill well before serving.

Serve each bowl of soup with a wedge of lemon at the side. If you like, top the soup with a spoonful of lightly whipped cream and sprinkle with a little nutmeg.

All recipes in these seasonal menus serve 12 people, so remember to triple the quantities of any recipes you use from another Volume.

Entrée

Salmon in Aspic

8–10 lb whole salmon, cleaned,
with head and tail left on
2 quarts court bouillon (made
with 6 cups water, 2 sliced
carrots, 1 large sliced onion
stuck with 1 clove, bouquet
garni, 6 peppercorns, and
2 cups white wine or 1½ cups
more water and ½ cup white
wine vinegar)
2 envelopes gelatin
½ cup cold water
2 egg whites
1 tablespoon white wine
vinegar
¼ cup sherry

For garnish
½ lb cooked, peeled shrimps
1 cucumber, scored with a fork
and sliced
bunch of watercress

Method
Make court bouillon and
reserve.

Wash salmon well, remove
gills, trim fins and cut the tail
in a 'V'. In a fish kettle or
large ovenproof dish arrange
salmon with the stomach
down and the tail curled
slightly. Pour over the court
bouillon while it is still warm.
Cover and poach salmon in
fish kettle for 40–50 minutes
over medium heat or in ovenproof dish in a moderate oven
(350°F) for 1 hour, basting
fish frequently, or until it
flakes easily. The liquid around
the fish should never boil,
only tremble. Let salmon cool
in court bouillon, then lift out
carefully and transfer to a
board or a large platter.

Boil the court bouillon to
reduce it by half; trail strips of
paper towel across surface to
remove any specks of fat.
Strain stock into a clean
scalded pan and leave to cool.

To make fish aspic: sprinkle
gelatin over the water in a
bowl and let stand 5 minutes
until spongy. Beat egg whites
until broken up and add to
cold fish stock with the wine
vinegar and sherry. Set pan
over moderate heat and whisk
backwards and downwards
with a balloon whisk so the
egg whites are thoroughly
mixed in. When hot, add
softened gelatin and continue
whisking until mixture just
starts to boil. Stop whisking
and let liquid rise to the top of
the pan, take from heat at
once and let liquid settle for
about 5 minutes. Bring again
to a boil, pull the pan aside
once more and let liquid
settle. At this point the egg
white 'filter' will have cracked
and the liquid beneath should
be clear. If not, repeat the
boiling process.

Carefully ladle the liquid
and 'filter' into a wet scalded
dish towel and leave to drain.
Let aspic cool before using.

When salmon is lukewarm,
snip skin along the top and
remove carefully, leaving the
skin on the head and the tail
intact. Cut through the backbone just below the head and
ease a knife along the bone.
Gently lift bone up and out
toward the tail. Cut it off
just before the tail and discard.

Spoon a little of the cool but
still liquid aspic over the bottom of a large platter; chill
until set. Lift salmon carefully with 2 spatulas and place
on prepared platter.

Arrange shrimps along top
of salmon and chill. Baste
with cool but still liquid aspic
and chill again, repeat coating
if necessary. Chill remaining
aspic until firm in a dampened,
clean ice cube tray or cake
pan, then turn out onto a
piece of wet brown or silicone
paper and chop it. Garnish
platter with cucumber slices,
watercress and chopped

aspic, and serve with mayonnaise Nantua and cucumber
salad.

*Cut backbone below the
head; ease a knife along the
bone, lift it out and cut it close
to the tail*

Accompaniments to entrée

Mayonnaise Nantua

¾ lb cooked, unpeeled shrimps
2 teaspoons paprika
3 cups olive oil
8 egg yolks
salt and pepper
6 tablespoons white wine
vinegar (or to taste)

Method
Peel shrimps, pound shells
with paprika and a little oil in a
mortar and pestle. Add
remaining oil and let stand
10–15 minutes. Alternatively,
work the shells, paprika and
oil in a blender and let stand.
Coarsely chop shrimps. Strain
oil through cheesecloth and
use it to make mayonnaise
with the egg yolks, seasoning
and vinegar. Stir in chopped
shrimps and season to taste.

Cucumber Salad

4 cucumbers, peeled and thinly
sliced
salt
1 cup vinaigrette dressing
3 tablespoons chopped chives

Method
Lightly sprinkle cucumber
slices with salt, press them
between 2 plates and leave in
a cool place for 1 hour to draw
out the juices (dégorger).
Drain, rinse slices with cold
water and pat dry.

Arrange slices in a large
serving dish and spoon over
the vinaigrette dressing.
Sprinkle with the chopped
chives and serve chilled.

Garnish platter of salmon in aspic with cucumber, watercress and chopped aspic

Dessert

Autumn Menu

Appetizer

Entrée

Pecan Parfait with Peaches

1½ cups coarsely chopped
   pecans
1½ cups sugar
1 cup water
6 egg whites
1½ cups heavy cream, whipped
   until it holds a soft shape
2 teaspoons vanilla

For topping
10–12 fresh peaches, peeled,
   pitted and sliced
4–6 tablespoons sugar
2 tablespoons kirsch (optional)
1 cup heavy cream, stiffly
   whipped (optional)
12 pecan halves (optional)

12 parfait glasses; pastry bag;
medium star tube (optional)

Method
Dissolve sugar in water over
low heat, bring to a boil and
cook steadily until syrup spins
a thread when a little is lifted
on a spoon (230°F–234°F on
a sugar thermometer). Stiffly
beat egg whites and pour
in hot sugar syrup, beating
constantly. Continue beating
until this meringue is cool and
very thick. Fold in whipped
cream with vanilla. Spoon
mixture into the parfait glasses
in layers with chopped pecans,
cover and freeze at least 4
hours or until parfait is firm.
   To make topping: sprinkle
peaches with sugar and kirsch,
if using; cover and leave to
macerate 1–2 hours.
   Just before serving, pile
peaches on top of pecan
parfait and, if you like, decorate each glass with a rosette
of whipped cream and a pecan
half.

Mushroom &
Watercress Soup

Chicken Crêpes
Chicory or Escarole
Salad
(see Volume 6)

Coffee Nut Slices

White wine – Graves (Bordeaux)
or Semillon (California)

TIMETABLE

Day before
Make soup but do not add
watercress; keep in refrigerator.
Make crêpes and filling,
roll them, cover and keep
in refrigerator.
Wash chicory or escarole
and store in plastic bag in
refrigerator; make dress-
ing.
Make and decorate cake
and keep covered in refrigerator.

Morning
Chop watercress for soup.
Coat crêpes with egg and
crumbs and arrange in
baking dish.
Cut cake in slices and
arrange on platter.

Just before serving
Reheat soup, add water-
cress and simmer 5–10
minutes.
Bake crêpes in a moder-
ately hot oven (375°F) for
20–25 minutes or until hot
and browned. Toss salad.

Mushroom and Watercress Soup

2 cups (½ lb) mushrooms
2 bunches of watercress,
   washed
6 tablespoons butter
2 medium onions, finely
   chopped
¼ cup flour
2½ quarts chicken stock
salt and pepper

Method
Wipe mushrooms with a
damp cloth; trim stems level
with caps. Chop stems and
half the caps very finely. In a
large saucepan melt butter
and add chopped mushrooms
and onion. Cover with wax
paper and a tight-fitting lid
and cook over low heat for
5–7 minutes or until vegetables are soft.
   Blend flour into the onion
and mushroom mixture, add 2
cups stock and bring to a boil,
stirring constantly. Add remaining stock, cover and
simmer 10–15 minutes. Slice
remaining mushroom caps
thinly, stir into the soup and
simmer 5 minutes. Pick over
watercress, discarding stems,
and chop finely. Add to soup
and cook 5–10 minutes
longer. Taste for seasoning
and serve.

**All recipes in these seasonal
menus serve 12 people, so
remember to triple the quantities of any recipes you use
from another Volume.**

Chicken Crêpes

3 cup quantity basic crêpe
   batter (see Volume 9)

For filling
2 cups diced, cooked chicken
2 cups diced cooked ham
¼ cup butter
¼ cup flour
2 cups chicken stock
½ cup heavy cream
squeeze of lemon juice
salt and pepper

To finish
3 eggs, beaten to mix
1 cup dry white breadcrumbs
½ cup butter
2 tablespoons chopped parsley

Makes about 36 crêpes.

Method
Make crêpe batter and let
stand 30 minutes.
   To make filling: in a saucepan melt the butter, stir in
flour, add stock and bring to
a boil, stirring. Simmer 2
minutes and stir in cream.
Bring just back to a boil, add
meats and lemon juice, taste
for seasoning and cool.
   Fry the crêpes, stacking
them one on top of the other.
Then place a generous spoonful of filling on each one, fold
over the edges and roll up
neatly. Cover and chill so the
rolls are firm.
   To finish: coat rolls in
beaten egg and cover with
breadcrumbs. Arrange crêpes
in a buttered baking dish and
dot with the butter. Bake in a
moderately hot oven (375°F)
for 20–25 minutes or until
crêpes are browned. Arrange
them on a platter, sprinkle
with parsley and serve with
chicory or escarole salad.

Dessert

Coffee Nut Slices

For sponge cake
4 eggs
¾ cup sugar
1 cup flour, sifted

For coffee butter frosting
1 tablespoon dry instant
   coffee, mixed to a paste
   with a little boiling water
¾ cup butter
1½ cups confectioners' sugar,
   sifted

For decoration
1 cup browned, slivered
   almonds
confectioners' sugar (for
   sprinkling)

Two 8 inch square cake pans

Method
Grease and flour cake pans
and sprinkle with sugar, discarding the excess. Set oven
at moderately hot (375°F).

Beat eggs in a bowl until
mixed, gradually beat in sugar
and set bowl over a pan of
hot water. Beat until mixture
is light and makes a ribbon
trail when the beater is lifted;
take bowl from pan and continue beating until mixture is
cool. If using an electric
mixer, no heat is necessary.
Fold in sifted flour and pour
batter into prepared pans.
Bake in heated oven for 15
minutes or until cake springs
back when lightly pressed
with a fingertip. Turn out onto
a wire rack to cool.

To prepare coffee butter
frosting: cream butter until
soft and stir in confectioners'
sugar, a little at a time, beating hard after each addition.
Add coffee paste to taste.

Trim off crusts from cakes,
then cut cakes in half across,

to make 4 strips. Spread 2
strips with a little frosting
and set the other 2 strips on
top of them. Spread tops and
sides of each cake thickly and
evenly with frosting, leaving
the ends bare. Press on
almonds and sprinkle with
confectioners' sugar. Put in
refrigerator to set frosting.
To serve, cut into 1 inch wide
slices.

**All recipes in these seasonal
menus serve 12 people, so
remember to triple the quantities of any recipes you use
from another Volume.**

Winter Menu

Oeufs à la Reine

*Beef Sauté Chasseur
Boiled Rice*

Cold Raspberry Soufflé

*Red wine – Gigondas
(Côte du Rhône)
or Zinfandel (California)*

TIMETABLE

Day before
Hard cook eggs and make
mayonnaise for oeufs à la
reine. Make filling and store
in airtight container. Keep
egg whites in a bowl of cold
water at room temperature.
Make beef sauté chasseur
and store in refrigerator.
Make raspberry soufflé,
cover tightly and chill.

Morning
Boil rice, drain and spread
in warm place to dry. Pile
in buttered heatproof dish
and cover with buttered
foil ready for reheating.
Decorate soufflé and let
stand at room temperature
for about 1 hour before
serving.
Arrange stuffed eggs, coat
with mayonnaise and
decorate with watercress.
Keep in refrigerator.

Just before serving
Reheat beef and rice in a
moderate oven (350°F)
for 35–45 minutes or until
very hot. Transfer to serving dishes, sprinkle beef
sauté chasseur with parsley
and serve.

Appetizer

Oeufs à la Reine
(Stuffed Eggs with
Chicken)

20–24 hard-cooked eggs
2 cups mayonnaise (for coating)
¼–½ cup milk or water (optional)
1 cup shredded almonds,
   browned (for sprinkling)
2 bunches of watercress (for
   garnish)

For filling
3 cups cooked chicken breast,
   finely chopped
⅓ cup white wine
3 teaspoons tarragon
about 1 cup mayonnaise
salt and pepper

Method
Mix the chicken with the white
wine and tarragon, cover and
leave to marinate 1–2 hours.

Peel the eggs, cut them in
half lengthwise and scoop out
the yolks. Work the yolks
through a sieve and mix half
with the marinated chicken
mixture; reserve the remaining yolks. Add enough mayonnaise to bind the mixture and
taste for seasoning. Fill the
egg whites and put two halves
together to reshape them. Cut
a thin slice off the side of each
egg, so they will sit firmly and
arrange them down one side
of two platters.

Thin the 2 cups mayonnaise
with milk or water to a consistency to coat the back of a
spoon and coat the eggs.
Sprinkle them with the
reserved egg yolks and top
with the browned almonds.
Garnish the dishes with
watercress.

Entrée

Beef Sauté Chasseur

6 lb lean chuck or round steak,
   cut in 2 inch cubes
$\frac{1}{4}$ cup oil
6 tablespoons butter
3 onions, finely chopped
3 cloves of garlic, crushed
3 tablespoons flour
5–6 cups beef stock
salt and pepper
bouquet garni
6 cups (1$\frac{1}{2}$ lb) mushrooms
3 cups white wine
2 tablespoons tomato paste
2 tablespoons chopped parsley
   (for garnish)

Method

In a large flameproof cas-
serole, heat the oil with $\frac{1}{4}$ cup
butter. Fry the meat, a few
pieces at a time over fairly
high heat, until browned on all
sides. Remove the meat, add
the onion and garlic and cook
slowly until soft but not
browned. Stir in the flour and
cook until well browned. Stir
in 5 cups of stock, bring to a
boil, add the meat with seasoning and bouquet garni,
cover and simmer on top of
the stove or in a moderate
oven (350°F) for 1$\frac{1}{2}$–2 hours
or until the beef is very tender.
Add more stock during cooking if the mixture looks dry
and stir from time to time.

Trim the mushroom stems
and quarter caps if large. In a
skillet melt remaining butter
and sauté mushrooms until
tender. Add wine and boil until
reduced by half; stir in tomato
paste.

Add the mushroom mixture
to the meat, cook 10 minutes
longer, remove the bouquet
garni and taste for seasoning. Transfer to a serving dish,
sprinkle with parsley and
serve with boiled rice.

Beef sauté chasseur, with mushrooms, is sprinkled with parsley

Dessert

Cold Raspberry Soufflé

3 cans (16 oz each) raspberries,
   or 6 packages frozen
   raspberries, thawed
3 envelopes gelatin
$\frac{1}{4}$ cup sugar
8 egg whites
1 quart heavy cream, whipped
   until it holds a soft shape

To decorate
candied violets (optional)
candied rose petals (optional)

*Glass bowl (4–4$\frac{1}{2}$ quart
   capacity)*

Method

Drain 1 cup juice from the
raspberries, reserving the
raspberries and remaining
juice. In a small pan put the
cup of juice and sprinkle over
gelatin. Let stand 5 minutes
until spongy, then dissolve
over a low heat. Stir gelatin
mixture into reserved raspberries and juice, add the
sugar and cool in refrigerator
or over a bowl of ice water
until on the point of setting,
stirring occasionally. Beat egg
whites until they hold a stiff
peak.

When raspberry mixture
starts to set, fold in three-
quarters of the whipped
cream, reserving the rest for
decoration. Fold in the beaten
egg whites and pour the mixture into a glass bowl. Chill

1–2 hours or until set.

To serve: take soufflé from
refrigerator $\frac{1}{2}$–1 hour before
serving, spread the top with
the remaining whipped cream
and mark a diamond pattern
with the tip of a small knife.
Decorate with candied violets
and rose petals, if you like.

Spiced chicken with orange (recipe is on page 25)

CHICKEN AND DUCK DISHES

Chicken and duck are birds of similar size but the resemblance ends there because they taste quite different. Chicken is adaptable – it can be cooked in almost any way and blends with flavors varying from mustard to mushrooms. The only problem with chicken is its tendency to be bland and dry; it must be cooked carefully and is particularly good with rich ingredients like cream, nuts and wine.

Duck, on the other hand, is rich and robust. Too much fat, not too little, is the difficulty with this bird and it must be cooked with this in mind. Roasting a duck in the oven or on a spit is excellent; or it can be cut in pieces and thoroughly fried to drain off as much fat as possible before simmering in a sauce. Since it is rich, wine and tart fruity flavors are good with duck – orange and cherries are famous combinations but lemon or fresh peaches are equally good.

Chickens vary enormously in size – a small 2–2$\frac{1}{2}$ lb bird serves two and large birds of 4–5 lb serve five to six people. Ducks are deceptive as a high proportion of their weight is bone and fat; a 4–5 lb duck serves only four people.

Instructions for cutting up and carving poultry were included in Volume 1.

Chicken trois frères is served with peach and ginger salad

HOT CHICKEN DISHES

Chicken Trois Frères

3½–4 lb roasting chicken
2–3 sprigs of fresh rosemary or
  1 teaspoon dried rosemary
¼ cup butter
½ cup white wine
1 cup chicken stock

For sauce
1½ tablespoons olive oil
1 tablespoon chopped onion
1 tablespoon chopped carrot
1 tablespoon flour
½ teaspoon tomato paste
1½ cups chicken stock

For garnish
12–16 small onions, blanched
  and peeled
2 cups (½ lb) mushrooms,
  quartered
salt and pepper
pinch of ground mace
1 tablespoon chopped parsley
  (optional)

Trussing needle and string

Method
Set oven at hot (400°F).
Put the rosemary with ½ tablespoon butter inside the bird. Truss it, spread the breast and legs with the remaining butter and put it in a roasting pan with wine and ½ cup stock. Cover with a piece of foil, but do not tuck it down. Roast in heated oven, basting often and turning the chicken so it cooks evenly, for 1 hour or until it is almost tender.
To make the sauce: heat the oil in a saucepan and fry the onion and carrot until begin-

ning to brown. Stir in the flour and cook, stirring, until a rich brown. Add the tomato paste and stock and simmer 20–25 minutes.
Take out the chicken and cut it into 5 pieces, discarding trussing strings. Put it in a casserole with the onions, mushrooms, seasoning and mace and keep warm. Add remaining stock to roasting pan and heat, stirring, to dissolve the pan juices. Boil well and strain into sauce, bring to a boil, taste for seasoning and strain over the chicken. Cover the pan, lower oven heat to moderate (350°F) and bake the chicken for 20–25 minutes or until very tender. Sprinkle with parsley, if you like, and serve with peach and ginger salad.

Chicken or Duck Stock

When cooking a whole chicken or duck make stock from the giblets (neck, gizzard, heart and feet, if available); never add the liver because it gives a bitter flavor. The liver is best used for making pâté or sautéed for a snack.
Heat a heavy saucepan with enough fat almost to cover the base; then add giblets and 1 onion, halved and washed but not peeled, and fry over a high heat until lightly browned. Remove pan from heat and add 1 quart cold water. Add ¼ teaspoon salt, a few peppercorns and a bouquet garni. Cover and simmer gently for 1–2 hours.

Peach and Ginger Salad

3 fresh peaches
¼ cup candied ginger, thinly
  sliced
1 Bibb lettuce or 1 heart of
  Boston lettuce, separated
  into leaves
1 tablespoon chopped parsley
  (for garnish)

For dressing
salt
black pepper, freshly ground
juice of ½ lemon
2 tablespoons olive oil

Method
To make the dressing: mix seasoning with lemon juice and whisk in the oil until the dressing thickens slightly. Add the sliced ginger.
A short time before serving, scald, peel and pit the peaches and slice them into the dressing; toss carefully to coat the slices.
Arrange the lettuce leaves around a dish or shallow salad bowl and spoon the peach mixture into the center. Sprinkle with parsley and serve with chicken trois frères.

Chicken Paulette

3½–4 lb roasting chicken, cut
  in pieces, or 5–6 chicken
  pieces
1 tablespoon olive oil
2 tablespoons butter

For mirepoix
8 scallions, trimmed and cut in
  ½ inch slices
1 carrot, diced
4 mushrooms, coarsely
  chopped
pinch of saffron, soaked in
  2 tablespoons boiling water
  for 30 minutes
pinch of ground ginger
¼ cup sherry
1 cup chicken stock
1 teaspoon arrowroot, mixed to
  a paste with 1 tablespoon
  water
¾ cup heavy cream
1 tablespoon Dijon-style
  mustard

Method
Heat oil and butter in a flameproof casserole and brown chicken pieces on all sides. Remove them.
To prepare the mirepoix: put scallions, carrot and mushrooms in casserole, lower heat, cover and cook gently for 4–5 minutes. Replace chicken pieces, add saffron liquid, ginger, sherry and stock, cover and simmer 30-40 minutes until chicken pieces are very tender. Transfer them to a platter and keep warm.
Boil sauce for 2–3 minutes or until well-flavored. Thicken by stirring in arrowroot paste and bringing just to a boil. Stir in cream and mustard, bring almost to a boil, taste for seasoning and spoon over chicken. Serve at once.

Poulet à l'Estragon
(Chicken with Tarragon)

3½–4 lb roasting chicken
3–4 slices of bacon
  (for barding)
1 onion, sliced
1 carrot, sliced
1 stalk of celery, sliced
few sprigs of parsley
5–6 cups chicken stock (made
  with giblets and 1 veal bone)
½ cup white wine

For sauce
bunch of fresh tarragon or
  1½ tablespoons dried
  tarragon
3 tablespoons butter
1 tablespoon flour
2½ cups stock (see method)
3 egg yolks
3 tablespoons heavy cream

Method
Make chicken stock, adding 1 veal bone and simmering 3–4 hours before straining.

Tie the slices of bacon over the breast of the chicken to bard it and set the bird on the sliced onion, carrot and celery in a kettle. Add sprigs of parsley, pour over the prepared stock to cover the chicken and add the wine. Cover the pan, bring slowly to a boil, skim well, and simmer gently, with the lid half on, for ¾–1 hour or until no pink juice runs out when the thigh of the chicken is pierced with a skewer. Strain and reserve the stock and keep the chicken warm in the pan.

To make the sauce: add the fresh tarragon and its stalks to reserved stock, reserving half the leaves, or add 1 tablespoon dried tarragon. Boil the stock until reduced to about 2½ cups, then strain it. Chop the reserved fresh tarragon leaves, if used.

Melt the butter, stir in the flour and cook until straw-colored. Pour in the stock and bring to a boil, stirring. Boil until reduced to the consistency of light cream. Mix the egg yolks with the cream, add a little of the hot sauce and stir this liaison back into the remaining sauce. Heat gently, stirring, until the sauce thickens slightly, but do not boil or it will curdle. Add the reserved tarragon leaves or the ½ tablespoon dried tarragon and taste sauce for seasoning.

Carve the chicken or leave it whole and arrange on a platter. Coat the chicken with sauce, serving the rest separately.

Poulet Poché au Vin Blanc
(Chicken Poached in White Wine)

3½–4 lb roasting chicken
1 carrot, sliced
1 onion, sliced
bouquet garni
6 peppercorns
2 cups white wine
salt
¼ cup butter
¼ cup flour
½ cup heavy cream
2 egg yolks (optional)
1 tablespoon chopped parsley
  or chives (for sprinkling)
3 thick slices of white bread,
  crusts removed and cut in
  ¾ inch cubes (for croûtons)

Method
Put the chicken in a kettle with the carrot, onion, bouquet garni, peppercorns, white wine, a very little salt and enough water to cover. Cover the pan and poach the chicken for ¾–1 hour, or until no pink juice runs out when the thigh is pierced with a skewer.

For the croûtons: bake the bread cubes in a moderate oven (350°F) for 10–20 minutes until lightly browned. (Time depends very much on the freshness of the bread.)

When the chicken is done, transfer it to a platter and keep warm. Strain the cooking stock and boil it until reduced to about 2½ cups. In a saucepan melt the butter, stir in the flour and cook to a pale straw color. Pour in the reduced stock and bring to a boil, stirring constantly. Simmer 5 minutes or until the sauce coats the back of a spoon. Stir the cream into the egg yolks (if using), stir a little hot sauce into this liaison and add the liaison to the remaining sauce. Reheat gently until the sauce thickens slightly, but do not boil. If using only cream, add it directly to the sauce. Taste the sauce for seasoning, spoon a little over the chicken to coat it and serve the rest separately. Sprinkle the chicken with parsley or chives, pile the croûtons around the edge and serve.

Mango Chicken

3½–4 lb roasting chicken, cut
  in pieces
1 fresh mango, peeled and cut
  in slices, or 1 can (14 oz)
  canned mango slices,
  drained
¼ cup seasoned flour (made
  with ¼ teaspoon salt and
  pinch of pepper)
¼ cup butter
2 medium onions, finely sliced
1–1½ cups chicken stock (see
  page 21)
salt and pepper
1 cup heavy cream

Method
Coat the chicken pieces with the seasoned flour. In a skillet heat the butter and, when foaming, put in chicken pieces, skin sides down, and brown slowly on all sides; remove them and keep warm.

Add onions to the pan and cook gently until beginning to brown, add the sliced mango and continue cooking until golden brown. Replace the chicken pieces, pour in 1 cup stock, season, cover the pan and simmer gently for 30–35 minutes or until chicken pieces are very tender; add more stock if the mixture looks dry.

When cooked, stir in the cream, bring just to a boil, taste for seasoning and serve mango chicken with boiled rice.

Chicken and duck dishes

Chicken poached in white wine is served with a cream sauce spooned over and croûtons piled around

For cuisses de poulet Xérès: the stuffed chicken legs are served with a cream sauce and garnished with glazed carrots

Cuisses de Poulet Xérès

8 chicken thighs and legs
2 shallots, finely chopped
5 tablespoons butter
$\frac{1}{4}$ cup fresh white breadcrumbs
3–4 tablespoons chicken stock
salt and pepper
pinch of ground mace or
    nutmeg
1 large onion, sliced
1 stalk of celery, sliced
bouquet garni
2 cups well-flavored stock

For white sauce
3 tablespoons butter
3 tablespoons flour
2 cups stock (see method)
$\frac{1}{2}$ cup heavy cream

For garnish
2 medium carrots
1 tablespoon butter
$\frac{1}{4}$ cup sherry or Madeira

Method

With a small pointed knife, remove the bones from the chicken thighs and legs, scraping the bones clean without slitting the meat. Grind or finely chop 2 thighs, discarding the skin. Cook the shallot in 3 tablespoons butter until soft, cool and add to the ground or chopped chicken with the breadcrumbs. Work well until smooth, beat in the 3–4 tablespoons chicken stock a little at a time and season highly with salt, pepper and mace or nutmeg. Fill this mixture into the boned chicken pieces and tie each with string.

Melt the remaining 2 tablespoons butter in a flameproof casserole, add the sliced vegetables, cover and cook gently for 7–8 minutes until they begin to brown. Set chicken on top, add bouquet garni and pour on the stock. Season well, cover with buttered foil, add the lid and bring to a boil. Braise in a moderate oven

(350°F) for 50–60 minutes or until the chicken is tender.

Take out the chicken pieces and keep them warm. Strain the cooking stock and boil until it is reduced to 2 cups.

To make the sauce: melt the butter, stir in the flour and cook until straw-colored. Cool a little and stir in the reserved stock. Bring to a boil, stirring, and simmer gently until the sauce is glossy and the consistency of heavy cream.

Cut the outer (orange) part of the carrots into julienne strips, discarding the core. Put them in a pan with the butter and sherry or Madeira, cover and simmer 10 minutes or until the carrots are tender. Add the carrots and their liquid to the sauce and stir in the heavy cream. Season to taste and keep warm.

Untie the strings from the chicken pieces, arrange chicken on a hot serving dish and spoon over the sauce. Serve with glazed carrots and boiled rice.

Tie boned and stuffed chicken pieces before braising them

Bone the chicken pieces to make cuisses de poulet Xérès

Spiced Chicken with Orange

$3\frac{1}{2}$–4 lb roasting chicken,
    cut in pieces, or 5–6 chicken
    pieces
1 teaspoon ground allspice
$\frac{1}{2}$ teaspoon ground cumin
$\frac{1}{2}$ teaspoon ground ginger
$\frac{1}{2}$ teaspoon ground cinnamon
2 tablespoons oil
1 tablespoon butter
1 tablespoon flour
$1\frac{1}{2}$ cups chicken stock
1 clove of garlic, crushed
salt and pepper
grated rind and juice of 1 orange
$\frac{1}{4}$ cup apricot jam
1 cup rice, boiled (for serving)

Method

Mix the allspice, cumin, ginger and cinnamon and rub into the chicken pieces. Cover and keep them in the refrigerator 2–3 hours or overnight.

In a flameproof casserole heat the oil and butter and fry the chicken over fairly low heat until golden brown on all sides. Sprinkle in the flour, then add the stock, garlic and seasoning, cover and bake in a moderate oven (350°F) or simmer on top of the stove for 30–40 minutes or until the chicken pieces are very tender. Transfer them to a plate.

Stir the orange juice into the apricot jam, add this mixture to the sauce and cook gently, stirring, until the sauce is syrupy. Taste the sauce for seasoning, replace the pieces of chicken and leave on a very low heat for 5 minutes for the flavors to mellow.

Arrange the cooked rice in a ring on a platter, put the chicken pieces on the center and spoon over the sauce. Sprinkle the rice with the grated orange rind.

Persian Chicken

3½–4 lb roasting chicken, cut in pieces
3 tablespoons oil
3 onions, sliced in rounds
3 tomatoes, peeled, sliced and seeded
1½ teaspoons tomato paste
1 cup chicken stock (see page 21)
salt and pepper
½ cup slivered almonds, soaked in warm water for 1 hour
½ cup currants or raisins, soaked in warm water for 1 hour
2 tablespoons butter

Method

In a skillet heat 2 tablespoons oil and fry the onions until lightly browned. Add the tomatoes, cook 3–4 minutes, then stir in the tomato paste, stock and seasoning. Simmer 20–30 minutes until well reduced and thickened. Drain the almonds and currants or raisins, add them to the tomato mixture and cook 10 minutes longer.

Meanwhile heat the remaining oil and butter in a shallow flameproof casserole and gently fry the chicken pieces for 25–30 minutes or until browned on all sides and tender. Spoon over the tomato and almond sauce, simmer 4–5 minutes longer, taste for seasoning and serve with buttered zucchini and pilaf.

Poulet Sauté au Citron
(Sauté of Chicken with Lemon)

2 broiling chickens (2–2½ lb each) split, with backbone removed
3 tablespoons butter
salt and pepper
½ cup white wine
1 cup well-flavored chicken stock (see page 21)
lemon fritters (for serving)

Method

In a large skillet or sauté pan heat the butter and brown the birds on both sides over low heat. Season well, add the wine and stock, cover and simmer 20–25 minutes or until the chickens are very tender.

Arrange the chickens on a platter, boil the cooking liquid until well reduced, taste for seasoning and spoon over the chickens. Serve with lemon fritters and boiled new potatoes tossed in butter and chopped parsley.

Lemon Fritters

Boil 2 lemons for 30 minutes. Drain them and cut in wedges or thick slices. Spoon over 2 tablespoons vinaigrette dressing and let marinate 1–2 hours. Make a fritter batter with 2 tablespoons flour, pinch of salt, 1 egg yolk, ½ tablespoon oil, ¼ cup milk. Cover and let stand 30 minutes. Just before using, fold in 1 egg white, stiffly whipped. Drain the slices of lemon, dip in the fritter batter and fry in hot deep fat (375°F on a fat thermometer) until golden brown. Drain on paper towels and serve at once.

To make lemon fritters, dip lemon slices in batter and gently lower them into hot deep fat, then fry until golden brown

Sauté of chicken with lemon is served with lemon fritters and new potatoes tossed in chopped parsley

Chicken vinaigrette with asparagus

COLD CHICKEN DISHES

Chicken Vinaigrette with Asparagus

3½–4 lb roasting chicken
1½ lb fresh asparagus or
   2 packages frozen asparagus
   (for garnish)
1 carrot
1 onion
bouquet garni
salt
6 peppercorns

For dressing
3 eggs
3 tablespoons white wine
   vinegar
1 shallot or scallion, finely
   chopped
1 tablespoon chopped parsley
1 teaspoon chopped chives
salt
black pepper, freshly ground
6 tablespoons olive oil
2–3 tablespoons light cream
   (optional)
pinch of sugar (optional)

Two cucumbers can be substituted for asparagus in this recipe. Peel, seed and cut them in julienne strips; blanch for 1 minute in boiling salted water.

Method
Put the chicken in a kettle with carrot, onion, bouquet garni, a little salt, peppercorns and water to cover. Cover pan and poach chicken ¾–1 hour or until no pink juice runs out when thigh is pierced with a skewer. Let cool in the liquid, then drain and carve neatly into 5–6 pieces, discarding skin. Arrange chicken on a platter.

Cook fresh asparagus, if used, drain, refresh and drain again (see box) or cook frozen asparagus according to package directions. Prepare cucumber as directed.

To make dressing: hard cook the eggs for 3½ minutes, peel them and scoop the yolks carefully into a bowl. Beat in the vinegar, shallot or scallion, herbs, salt and pepper and gradually add the oil, beating constantly. Chop egg whites and stir them, with cream, if used, into the dressing. Taste for seasoning, adding a pinch of sugar, if you like.

Spoon the dressing over the chicken and arrange the cooked asparagus or cucumber on the platter.

To Cook Fresh Asparagus

Trim the white part from the asparagus stalks so they are the same length. Rinse them in cold water and with a vegetable peeler remove the tough skin from the lower ends of the stems. Tie asparagus stalks in several bundles and stand these, stems down, in 1–2 inches boiling salted water in an asparagus cooker or tall pan. Cover and simmer 8–10 minutes or until the green tips are just tender. Lift bundles carefully from pan, drain on paper towels and remove strings.

Chicken with Curry Mayonnaise

3½–4 lb roasting chicken
1 carrot, sliced
1 onion, sliced
bouquet garni
6 peppercorns
salt
bunch of watercress (for
   garnish)
rice salad (for serving)

For curry mayonnaise
2 teaspoons curry powder
2 cups mayonnaise
2 teaspoons oil
½ onion, finely chopped
1 cup tomato juice
1½ tablespoons apricot jam
¼ cup cream, whipped until it
   holds a soft shape

Method
Put the chicken in a kettle with the carrot, onion, bouquet garni, peppercorns, a little salt and water to cover. Cover the pan and poach the chicken for ¾–1 hour or until no pink juice runs out when the thigh is pierced with a skewer. Let cool in the liquid until tepid, remove chicken from liquid and chill.

To make the curry mayonnaise: heat the oil, add the onion and fry gently until soft but not brown. Add the curry powder and cook gently, stirring, for 2 minutes. Stir in the tomato juice and apricot jam, simmer 5 minutes and strain.

Let cool, then beat the curry mixture into the mayonnaise; fold in the lightly whipped cream.

Cut up the chicken into 5–6 pieces, discarding the skin, and arrange it on a platter. Coat the chicken with the mayonnaise and garnish the platter with watercress. Serve rice salad separately.

Rice Salad

1¼ cups long grain rice
1 cucumber, peeled and diced
1 large carrot, diced
1 cup diced green beans
1 cup shelled fresh peas or
   1 package frozen peas,
   thawed
1 red bell pepper, cored, seeded
   and diced
2 medium tomatoes, peeled,
   seeded and cut in strips
½ cup vinaigrette dressing
salt

Method
Cook the rice in boiling salted water for 12–15 minutes, drain, rinse with hot water and spread out in an airy place to dry.

Sprinkle the cucumber with salt, cover and let stand 30 minutes to draw out the juices (dégorger), then rinse and dry on paper towels.

Cook the carrot, beans and peas in boiling salted water for 6–8 minutes or until just tender, then drain, refresh and drain again. Blanch the pepper for 2 minutes in boiling salted water, drain, refresh and drain again.

Add all the vegetables and tomatoes to the rice and toss with the vinaigrette dressing with 2 forks. Arrange on a platter.

Barossa Chicken

3½–4 lb roasting chicken
1½ cups (½ lb) seedless green
    grapes
¼ cup butter
salt
black pepper, freshly ground
½ cup white wine
1 head of lettuce, shredded
2 tablespoons olive oil
1 cup whole blanched almonds,
    split in half lengthwise
squeeze of lemon juice

For dressing
½ cup white wine
juice of ½ lemon
¾ cup olive oil
1 tablespoon mixed chopped
    herbs (parsley, mint, chives)

This recipe is named after an Australian vineyard – Barossa.

Method
Set oven at hot (400°F).

Put half the butter inside the chicken, season inside, truss it and spread the remaining butter on the breast. Set chicken in a roasting pan, pour around ½ cup white wine, cover loosely with foil and roast in heated oven for 1¼ hours or until the chicken is tender and no pink juice runs out when the thigh is pierced with a skewer. During cooking turn it from one side to another, then onto its back and baste often. Let cool, then carve chicken and arrange on the shredded lettuce on a platter. Reserve juice from roasting, discarding all fat.

In a pan heat the oil and fry the almonds gently until browned; drain them on paper towels and sprinkle with a little salt. Sprinkle the grapes with a little lemon juice and reserve.

To make dressing: boil the wine until reduced by half, then let cool. Mix it with the lemon juice, olive oil and herbs and reserved juice from roasting the chicken. Add the grapes. Just before serving, spoon dressing over chicken and scatter with almonds.

Chicken Mille Feuilles

1 cup finely ground, cooked
    chicken
2 cup quantity puff pastry
    (see Volume 8)
3 tablespoons butter, creamed
béchamel sauce, made with
    2 tablespoons butter,
    2 tablespoons flour, 1 cup
    milk (infused with slice of
    onion, 6 peppercorns, blade
    of mace and bay leaf)
1–2 tablespoons heavy cream
salt and pepper
1 cup quantity mayonnaise
    collée (see box)

For garnish
1 canned truffle, drained and
    sliced, or 2 mushrooms,
    sliced and cooked in 2
    tablespoons water with a
    squeeze of lemon juice
1 cup cool but still liquid aspic

If chicken mille feuilles is to be served at once, the aspic coating can be omitted.

Method
Make the béchamel sauce, cover tightly and let cool. Set the oven at hot (425°F).

Roll out the pastry dough as thinly as possible to a large rectangle. Lay this on a dampened baking sheet, letting the dough come slightly over the edge. Prick dough well all over with a fork and chill 10 minutes. Bake in heated oven for 10–15 minutes or until browned. Loosen the pastry with a spatula and turn it over. Bake 5 minutes longer, then transfer to a rack to cool.

When cold, trim the edges and cut remaining pastry into 3 strips, each about 3 inches wide; lightly crush pastry trimmings.

In a mortar and pestle pound the chicken and gradually beat in the butter. When smooth, stir in the béchamel sauce and cream and season well. Spread the mixture on 2 strips of pastry, reserving the third strip.

Make the mayonnaise collée, spoon it to coat the reserved pastry strip and chill until set. Decorate with sliced truffle or mushrooms and coat with cool but still liquid aspic. Chill until firmly set, then lay this strip on top of the mille feuilles. Press the crushed pastry trimmings along the sides and set on a silver platter or board covered with a white napkin. To serve, cut in 2 inch slices.

Mayonnaise Collée

Sprinkle ½ envelope gelatin over ¼ cup cool but still liquid aspic and let stand 5 minutes until spongy.

Dissolve gelatin mixture over a pan of hot water and stir into 1 cup mayonnaise. Use when cool but still pourable.

HOT DUCK DISHES

Canard aux Navets
(Roast Duck with Turnips)

4–5 lb duck
peeled rind of 1 lemon
salt and pepper
1 cup duck stock (see page 21)
1½ cups Espagnole sauce
    (see Volume 2)
1 cup white wine
juice of ½ lemon

For garnish
6–8 small white turnips, peeled
    and quartered
2 tablespoons butter
1 tablespoon sugar
10–12 small onions, blanched
    and peeled

Trussing needle and string

Method
Put the lemon rind inside the duck, sprinkle the inside with seasoning and truss it. Set on a rack in a roasting pan, pour around the stock and prick the skin all over to release the fat. Roast in a hot oven (400°F) for about 1½ hours or until the skin is crisp and browned and the thigh of the bird is tender when pierced with a fork. During cooking turn the bird from one side to another, then onto its back and baste occasionally; discard excess fat as it gathers in the bottom of the pan.

Make the Espagnole sauce.

To prepare garnish: blanch the turnips and drain them. Melt the butter in a flameproof casserole, add the turnips,

For canard aux navets, roast duck is garnished with caramelized onions and turnips

sprinkle with sugar and cook over very low heat, shaking the pot from time to time, for 10–15 minutes or until the turnips are almost tender and the sugar has begun to cara-melize. Add the blanched onions and cook 8–10 min-utes longer or until the onions and turnips are tender and glazed with caramel.

When cooked, transfer the duck to a platter, discard trussing strings and keep warm. Discard the fat from the pan and dissolve the pan juices in the wine and lemon juice, boiling well. Strain the mixture into the Espagnole sauce and boil rapidly until glossy and the consistency of light cream. Spoon a little sauce over the duck, garnish the platter with turnips and onions and serve remaining sauce separately.

Roast Duck with Orange

4–5 lb duck, with the liver
   and giblets
3 navel oranges
salt
black pepper, freshly ground
1 cup duck stock (see page 21)
2 tablespoons brandy
$\frac{1}{2}$ cup red wine

For sauce
$\frac{1}{4}$ cup sugar
$\frac{1}{4}$ cup water
$\frac{1}{4}$ cup vinegar
3 tablespoons oil
1 onion, diced
1 carrot, diced
$1\frac{1}{2}$ tablespoons flour
2–$2\frac{1}{2}$ cups duck stock
$\frac{1}{2}$ cup red wine
2 tablespoons brandy (optional)

Trussing needle and string

Method

Thinly peel the rind from the oranges and place a few strips inside the duck. Sprinkle the inside of the duck with seasoning, truss it and place on a rack in a roasting pan. Pour around 1 cup stock and prick the skin all over to release the fat. Roast in a hot oven (400°F) for about $1\frac{1}{2}$ hours or until the skin is crisp and browned and the thigh of the bird is tender when pierced with a fork. During cooking turn the bird from one side to another, then onto its back and baste occasionally; discard excess fat as it gathers in the bottom of the pan.

To make the sauce: for the caramel, heat the sugar in the water until dissolved, then bring to a boil and boil steadily to a rich brown caramel. Take from the heat, cover the hand holding the pan and at once pour in the vinegar.
Watchpoint: stand back because the vapor from the vinegar will make your eyes

sting. Heat the mixture gently until the caramel is dissolved.

Cut the neck and gizzard of the duck into chunks and in a heavy-based pan fry them in oil until well browned. Take out, add the diced onion and carrot and cook over low heat until just beginning to brown. Stir in the flour and cook until browned. Pour in 2 cups stock and bring to a boil, stirring. Add $\frac{1}{2}$ cup of the red wine, browned giblets, caramel mixture and remaining orange rind and simmer the sauce, uncovered, for 40–50 minutes. Add half the remaining cold stock, bring to a boil, skim well and simmer 5 minutes. Add remaining stock and repeat skimming. Finely chop duck liver, add to the sauce and simmer 5 minutes. Strain the sauce and reserve.

With a serrated-edge knife, cut the skin and pith from the oranges and segment them, discarding the membrane. Put the segments in a small pan with 2 tablespoons brandy.

When the duck is cooked, transfer to a platter, discard trussing strings and keep warm. Gently heat the orange segments.

Discard the fat from the roasting pan and dissolve the pan juices in the $\frac{1}{2}$ cup red wine, boiling it well. Strain this liquid into the sauce, add the brandy, if using, bring just to a boil and taste for seasoning. Spoon a little sauce over the duck and garnish the platter with orange segments. Serve the remaining sauce separately.

Roast Duck with Peaches

Roast the duck and make the orange sauce as for duck with orange but serve with a garnish of caramelized fresh peaches.

To caramelize peaches: scald, halve, pit and peel 4–6 ripe peaches. Set them, cut side down, in a baking dish, sprinkle with 2 tablespoons dark brown sugar and 2 tablespoons brandy and dot with 2 tablespoons butter. Bake in a hot oven (400°F) with the duck for 10–15 minutes or until browned.

Roast Duck with Mint and Lemon

4–5 lb duck
1 tablespoon chopped fresh
   mint
1 teaspoon sugar
2 tablespoons butter, creamed
grated rind and juice of
   $\frac{1}{2}$ lemon
salt and pepper
1 cup duck stock (see page 21)

For garnish
$1\frac{1}{2}$ lemons, sliced
bunch of watercress

Trussing needle and string

Method

Mix half the chopped mint with the sugar, butter, grated lemon rind and seasoning. Put this mixture inside the duck and truss it.

Place the duck on a rack in a roasting pan, pour around half the stock and prick the skin all over to release the fat. Roast in a hot oven (400°F) for about $1\frac{1}{2}$ hours or until the skin is crisp and browned

and the thigh of the bird is tender when pierced with a fork. During cooking turn the bird from one side to another, then onto its back and baste occasionally; discard excess fat as it gathers in the bottom of the pan. When cooked, transfer the duck to a platter, discard trussing strings and keep warm.

Discard the fat from the pan and dissolve the pan juices in the remaining stock and the lemon juice. Bring it to a boil, season and strain. Add the remaining chopped mint to the sauce, taste for seasoning, and spoon it over the duck.

Garnish the platter with lemon slices and small bunches of watercress.

Roast Duck with Cherries

Cook the duck and make the orange sauce as for roast duck with orange, but serve it with cherry compote with port.

COLD DUCK DISHES

Duck with Pâté and Cherries

4–5 lb duck (with the liver and giblets)
salt and pepper
1 cup duck stock (see page 21)
$\frac{1}{3}$ cup red wine

For pâté
1 cup ($\frac{1}{2}$ lb) chicken livers and liver from duck
$\frac{1}{2}$ cup butter
1 medium onion, finely chopped
1 clove of garlic, crushed
small bouquet garni
black pepper, freshly ground
1 tablespoon brandy

To finish
2 cups cool but still liquid aspic
bunch of watercress
cherry compote with port (for serving)

Trussing needle and string

Method
Sprinkle the inside of the duck with seasoning and truss it. Set it on a rack in a roasting pan, pour around the stock and wine and add the giblets. Prick the skin all over to release the fat. Roast in a hot oven (400°F) for about 1$\frac{1}{2}$ hours or until the skin is crisp and browned and the thigh of the bird is tender when pierced with a fork. During cooking turn the bird from one side to another, then on its back and baste occasionally; discard excess fat as it gathers in the bottom of the pan.

To make the pâté: in a skillet heat 2 tablespoons butter and fry the onion with the garlic until just beginning to brown. Add the chicken and duck livers, bouquet garni, salt and black pepper and fry briskly for 3 minutes or until the livers are browned but still pink in the center. Cool, discard the bouquet garni and finely chop mixture or work it in a blender with a little of the remaining butter. Work the mixture through a sieve to remove the liver ducts. Cream the remaining butter and work it into the liver mixture. Add the brandy, taste for seasoning and pile the pâté on a serving dish to make a socle (platform) for the duck. Smooth it neatly and chill until firm.

Make the cherry compote. When the duck is cooked, let cool, then carve and arrange on the pâté. Chill it thoroughly, then brush or coat it with cool but still liquid aspic, adding a second coating, if necessary. Garnish the platter with watercress and serve with cherry compote with port.

Lemon Compote

Thinly peel rind from 1 lemon, cut in needle-like shreds and blanch in boiling water for 5 minutes, then drain. With a serrated-edge knife slice peel and pith from 3 lemons and slice the flesh in thin rounds, discarding all seeds.

Dip 2–3 fresh tarragon sprigs in boiling water and sprinkle leaves (or use 1 teaspoon of dried tarragon) over lemons. Heat 2 tablespoons sugar (or to taste) with 3 tablespoons water until dissolved, boil 2–3 minutes to a thick syrup and cool it. Pour it over lemons, cover and let stand at least 2 hours; if needed, add a little more sugar — the compote should be tart. Chill before serving.

Cherry Compote with Port

Put 1 lb tart red cherries, pitted, in a pan with 2 tablespoons sugar and pinch of ground cinnamon. Cover, cook slowly 5 minutes or until juice runs out; take from heat. Alternatively, use 1 can (16 oz) tart cherries, drained of all but a few tablespoons syrup.

Boil $\frac{1}{4}$ cup port until reduced by half, add grated rind and juice of 1 orange and juice from cherries; stir in $\frac{1}{4}$ cup red currant jelly and heat gently until melted. Add the cherries and heat until they are hot.

Duck with Lemon Compote

4–5 lb duck
2 sprigs of fresh rosemary, chopped, or 1 teaspoon dried rosemary
bunch of watercress (for garnish)
lemon compote (for serving)

For stuffing
2 slices of bacon, finely diced
4 mushrooms, chopped
liver from the duck
2 chicken livers
1 shallot, chopped
1 tablespoon chopped parsley
1 cup fresh white breadcrumbs
salt
black pepper, freshly ground
1 egg, beaten to mix

Trussing needle and string

Method
To make the stuffing: fry the bacon until crisp, drain off excess fat, stir in the chopped mushrooms, continue cooking 1 minute and let cool. Coarsely chop the livers and mix with the bacon and mushrooms, shallot, parsley, breadcrumbs, and plenty of seasoning. Add the egg to bind the mixture, put this into duck and truss it.

Set the duck on a rack in a roasting pan and prick the skin all over to release the fat. Sprinkle the bird with rosemary and roast in a hot oven (400°F) for about 1$\frac{3}{4}$ hours or until the skin is crisp and browned and the thigh of the bird is tender when pierced with a fork. During cooking turn the bird from one side to another, then on its back and baste occasionally; discard fat as it gathers in pan.

Let the duck cool, then carve it, arrange on a platter and pile the stuffing down one side. Garnish with watercress and serve the lemon compote, chilled, separately.

Sole Dorothea, coated with tomato-flavored sauce, is garnished with truffles (recipe is on page 38)

A CLASSIC MENU

Ginger & Grapefruit Cocktail
or
Mushrooms au Gratin

Fillets of Sole Dorothea
or
Escalopes de Veau Provençale
Mashed Potatoes

Bombe Diane

White wine – Oppenheimer (Germany)
or Sylvaner (California)

This menu combines superb examples of classic French cuisine, but it is easy to prepare with the help of the time-table. As entrée, there is a choice of sole fillets coated with a delicate, creamy tomato sauce and garnished with truffles, or escalopes of veal cooked with eggplant, tomatoes and ripe olives in the style of Provence. The molded iced dessert combines coffee ice cream with bananas and cream.

The delicate sauce for the sole calls for something out of the ordinary in the way of wine, and a dry white in the German tradition is an ideal choice. Try a vineyard wine from the town of Oppenheim, or one of its neighbors, in the Rheinhessen district. Alternatively, you might select a Sylvaner from one of the better growers in California's Napa Valley.

TIMETABLE

Day before
Make coffee ice cream for bombe and freeze. Make banana filling, complete bombe and freeze. *Or make crème beau rivage but do not add topping. Keep tightly covered in refrigerator.*
Make fresh tomato purée and béchamel sauce for the sole and keep, tightly covered, in refrigerator.

Morning
Prepare grapefruit but do not add ginger; cover and chill.
Prepare mushrooms, coat with sauce and leave ready for baking.
Cook eggplant mixture and peel potatoes for veal.
Cook rice for sole and leave in pan ready for reheating.
Add topping to crème beau rivage and leave at room temperature.

Assemble ingredients for final cooking from 12:15 for lunch around 1 p.m.

You will find that **cooking times** given in the individual recipes for these dishes have sometimes been adapted in the timetable to help you when cooking and serving this menu as a party meal.

Order of Work

12:15
Set oven at moderate (350°F) for sole and rice *or hot (400°F) for mushrooms. Boil potatoes for veal.*
Put ginger on grapefruit halves and place them in serving bowls; chill.
12:30
Poach sole in heated oven and reheat rice.
12:40
*Drain potatoes, mash, and leave covered with hot milk. Cook escalopes and reheat eggplant mixture on top of stove. Arrange on a platter and keep warm.
Finish mashed potatoes.*
12:45
Bake mushrooms in oven.
Spoon rice into mold and let stand in a warm place.
12:50
Turn out the rice mold on a platter but do not remove mold; arrange fish around mold.
Add cream and tomato purée to béchamel sauce. Keep warm over hot water.
1:00
Serve appetizer.
Remove ring mold and coat fish with sauce just before serving.
Unmold bombe Diane just before serving.

Ginger and Grapefruit Cocktail

2 large grapefruit
$\frac{1}{4}$ cup ginger preserves

4 coupe glasses or bowls

Method
To prepare grapefruit: using a grapefruit knife, remove the cores, then cut around the edges of the grapefruit between the flesh and the pith so the flesh is completely detached from the shell. Slip the knife down each side of the membrane dividing the grapefruit sections, then lift out all the membranes in one piece. Remove any seeds.
Put 1 tablespoon of the ginger preserves in the center of each grapefruit half. Chill and serve them in coupe glasses or bowls.

Mushrooms au Gratin

4 cups (1 lb) mushrooms
2–3 tablespoons butter
salt and pepper
pinch of ground mace
pinch of cayenne
2–3 tablespoons browned breadcrumbs mixed with 2–3 tablespoons grated Parmesan cheese (for sprinkling)

For white sauce
2 tablespoons butter
2 tablespoons flour
1 cup milk
$\frac{1}{3}$ cup heavy cream

Method
Set oven at hot (400°F).
Trim the stems of the mushrooms level with the caps; wipe them with a damp cloth. Fry mushrooms in the butter for 2–3 minutes or until they are tender. Spoon them into individual gratin dishes or a large baking dish. Sprinkle with salt, pepper and a pinch of ground mace and cayenne.
Make the white sauce and season. Stir in the heavy cream. Spoon the sauce over the mushrooms and sprinkle with the browned breadcrumbs mixed with the grated Parmesan cheese. Bake mushrooms in heated oven for 7–10 minutes or until the tops are browned.

A classic menu

After removing membranes and seeds, the grapefruit halves are topped with ginger preserves

Fillets of Sole Dorothea

1½ lb sole fillets
squeeze of lemon juice
salt and pepper

For rice
1 cup rice
1 small onion, finely chopped
2 tablespoons butter
pinch of saffron, infused in
    2 tablespoons boiling water
    for 30 minutes
1 cup fresh tomato purée
    (see box) or 1 can (8 oz)
    tomato purée
2–2½ cups chicken or veal stock

For sauce
béchamel sauce made with
    2 tablespoons butter,
    2 tablespoons flour and
    1 cup milk (infused with slice
    of onion, 6 peppercorns,
    blade of mace and bay leaf)
⅓ cup heavy cream
small can truffles (optional)

Ring mold (5 cup capacity)

Method
Set oven at moderate (350°F);
butter the mold.
    To prepare the rice: in a
flameproof casserole cook the
onion in the butter until soft
but not brown. Stir in the rice
and cook gently until the grains
look transparent. Strain the
saffron liquid into the rice and
add half the tomato purée and
2 cups stock. Season, bring to
a boil, cover and bake in heated
oven for 15 minutes. Add more
stock if the mixture looks dry
and continue baking 5–7 minutes longer or until the rice is
tender and all the liquid is
absorbed. Let stand 10 minutes, then stir lightly with a
fork and taste for seasoning.

Spoon rice into the pre-
pared mold, press down lightly
and keep warm.
    Fold sole fillets in half,
crosswise, and lay them in a
buttered baking dish. Pour
over enough water to cover,
add a squeeze of lemon juice
and a little salt, cover with
foil and poach in heated oven
for 10–12 minutes or until
sole flakes easily when tested
with a fork.
    To make sauce: first make
béchamel sauce and stir in
the cream. Add enough of the
remaining tomato purée to
give sauce a delicate tomato
flavor. If using truffles, cut
8–10 slices for decoration;
chop the rest. Stir in chopped
truffle and liquid from can;
taste for seasoning.
    Turn the rice mold out onto
the center of a platter. Drain
the sole fillets and arrange,
overlapping slightly, around
the rice. Spoon the sauce over
the fish and into center of rice
mold. Decorate with truffle
slices, if you like, and serve
at once.

*Arrange the sole fillets around
the rice mold and coat them
with tomato-flavored béchamel sauce*

**To Make Fresh
Tomato Purée**

For 1 cup: seed and
coarsely chop 2 large ripe
tomatoes. Put them in a
saucepan with a lightly
bruised clove of garlic,
bay leaf, slice of onion
and salt and freshly
ground black pepper.
Add about 1 tablespoon
butter, cover and cook
over a low heat, stirring
occasionally, for 12–15
minutes or until tomatoes
are a very thick pulp. Then
work pulp through a sieve.
Taste and adjust season-
ing, adding a little sugar if
you like. The pulp should
not have an acid taste.

Alternative
entrée

Escalopes de Veau Provençale

4–8 (about 1½ lb) veal escalopes
1 eggplant, sliced
2 tablespoons seasoned flour
  (made with pinch of salt and
  pinch of pepper)
salt and pepper
¼ cup olive oil (for frying)
1 clove of garlic, finely chopped
1 teaspoon tomato paste
½ cup white wine
4 tomatoes, peeled, quartered
  and seeded
8 ripe olives, pitted
1 tablespoon chopped parsley

Method

Sprinkle the eggplant slices with salt and let stand 30 minutes to draw out the juices (dégorger); then rinse and drain on paper towels.

Coat escalopes in seasoned flour. In a frying pan heat 2 tablespoons olive oil and sauté escalopes for 3–4 minutes on each side until golden brown, turning only once. Remove from the pan and keep warm.

Add garlic to the pan and sauté for 1 minute or until lightly browned, then stir in tomato paste and wine. Season, cover the pan and cook over a low heat for 7–8 minutes or until slightly thickened.

In another pan fry the eggplant slices in the remaining 2 tablespoons olive oil for 2–3 minutes on each side until golden brown. Add the tomatoes to the pan and simmer them with the eggplant for 5–6 minutes or until they are soft and pulpy. Stir in the olives and season.

Arrange escalopes in a warm serving dish, overlapping them slightly. Heat the sauce and spoon over them. Arrange the eggplant mixture at each end of the dish and sprinkle with chopped parsley. Serve with mashed potatoes.

Escalopes de veau Provençale are served with eggplant, tomato and ripe olives

Bombe Diane, filled with a banana and cream mixture, is a spectacular dessert

Dessert

Bombe Diane

For coffee ice cream
1–1½ tablespoons dry instant
    coffee
2½ cups milk
2 eggs
2 egg yolks
⅓ cup sugar
1 teaspoon vanilla extract
1 cup heavy cream, whipped
    until it holds a soft shape

For filling
4–5 bananas
1 tablespoon lemon juice or
    rum
1–2 tablespoons confectioners'
    sugar
½ cup heavy cream, whipped
    until it holds a soft shape

*Ice cream churn freezer
(optional); bombe mold or
metal bowl (1½ quart
capacity)*

Method
Stir a little of the milk into the
coffee until dissolved. Beat
the eggs with the egg yolks
until mixed and whisk in the
sugar until mixture is smooth
but does not start to thicken.
Scald the milk, let cool,
covered, and strain milk into
the egg mixture, stirring
vigorously. Cool, then strain
custard and add vanilla extract.
Cover and chill the mixture.
Stir in the whipped cream
and taste for flavor, adding
more vanilla if necessary.
Cover and chill the mixture
thoroughly, overnight if you
like.
Freeze the mixture in an ice
cream churn freezer or in ice
cube trays (see Volume 11).
When stiff, leave the ice
cream in the churn freezer or
ice trays for 1–2 hours or
until very firm. Chill bombe

mold and lid or metal bowl.
To make filling: slice bananas, sprinkle with lemon
juice or rum and confectioners'
sugar and fold in the lightly
whipped cream.
When ready, line or coat
the sides of the mold or bowl
with the ice cream. Fill the
center with the banana mixture, pressing down well so
no air pockets are left. Add
the lid and seal with shortening or cover the bowl with a
layer of wax paper, then a
layer of foil tied securely with
string.
Freeze the mold or bowl
for 2–3 hours in a freezer or
for 3–4 hours in a churn
freezer, if for use immediately; or store for 2–3 weeks
in a freezer.
To turn out, dip the mold
or bowl into cold water, wipe
the outside, remove the lid or
foil cover, replace it lightly
and dip again in cold water
up to the level of the lid or
cover. Dry again and invert
the mold or bowl onto a
chilled platter. If the bombe
will not turn out, wrap a warm
cloth around the mold or bowl
for 30 seconds.

*For bombe Diane, line the
bottom and sides of the mold
with ice cream*

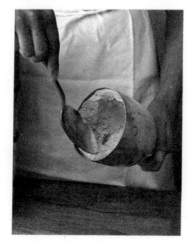

Alternative dessert

Crème Beau Rivage

3 tangerines or 2 oranges
8–10 sugar cubes
2 cups milk
1 envelope gelatin
3 egg yolks
¼ cup sugar
1 teaspoon arrowroot or
    cornstarch
1 egg white
½ cup cream, whipped until
    it holds a soft shape

To finish
¼ cup red currant jelly
3–4 tablespoons water

*Glass serving bowl (5 cup
    capacity)*

Method
Rub the sugar cubes over the
rind of the tangerines or
oranges until saturated with
zest (oil). Heat the sugar
cubes with the milk until
they are dissolved.
Squeeze the juice from 1
tangerine or ½ orange and
measure ¼ cup juice. Sprinkle
over the gelatin and let stand
5 minutes or until spongy.
Peel the remaining tangerines
or oranges and slice them.
Beat the egg yolks with the
sugar and arrowroot or cornstarch until thick and light,
stir in the hot milk mixture
and return the custard to the
pan. Heat gently, stirring,
until the custard thickens
enough to coat the back of the
spoon.
Add the softened gelatin to
the hot custard and stir until
dissolved. Let cool, stirring
occasionally. Stiffly whip the
egg white. Set the pan of

custard over a bowl of ice
water and stir until it is on the
point of setting. At once fold
in the lightly whipped cream,
followed by the egg white.
Pour the crème into a glass
serving bowl, cover tightly and
chill at least 2 hours or until
set.
An hour or two before serving, arrange the tangerine or
orange slices, overlapping, on
top of the crème. Melt the red
currant jelly with the water,
stirring until smooth, let cool
to tepid and spoon over the
top of the crème to coat both
fruit and crème.

Lamb chop dishes are: with herbs (top left); Reform (below), and Alsacienne with potatoes and mushrooms, and cabbage

CLASSIC ENTREES (3)

Classic entrées are ideal for present-day entertaining. They combine luxury cuts of meat — tournedos steaks, veal escalopes, lamb loin chops and chicken — with a colorful vegetable garnish and often a rich accompanying sauce. The individual portions of meat and the garnish around them on the platter make the dish both attractive and easy to serve.

More classic entrées were given in Volumes 12, 15 and 17.

Lamb Chops Reform

8 loin or rib lamb chops
¼ cup seasoned flour (made
  with ¼ teaspoon salt, pinch
  of pepper)
1 egg, beaten to mix
½ cup dry white breadcrumbs
2 thin slices of cooked ham,
  finely chopped
2 tablespoons oil
2 tablespoons butter

For garnish
1 medium carrot, cut in
  julienne strips
4 gherkin pickles, sliced
white of 1 hard-cooked egg,
  cut in strips
4 mushrooms, cut in ¼ inch
  slices
2–3 tablespoons stock
1 tablespoon butter
salt and pepper

For sauce
1 teaspoon red currant jelly
1 tablespoon port
1½ cups Espagnole sauce
  (see Volume 2)
small pinch of cayenne

This dish was created for the
Reform Club of London,
England, by the famous chef
Alexis Soyer in the middle of
the 19th century.

Method
Trim the fat and meat from the
ends of the chops to expose
about 1 inch of bone, then
scrape the bone ends clean.
Flatten chops slightly with a
mallet, coat them with seasoned flour, brush with
beaten egg and roll in the dry
white breadcrumbs mixed
with the finely chopped ham,
pressing the mixture in well
with a spatula.

To prepare garnish: cook
the carrot in boiling salted
water for 5–6 minutes until
just tender and drain. Put the
carrot, gherkin pickles, egg

white, mushrooms and stock
in a pan, cover and heat gently
until very hot and the mushrooms are tender. Add 1
tablespoon butter, season and
keep warm.

To make the sauce: melt
the red currant jelly in the port,
stir into the Espagnole sauce,
bring to a boil, add cayenne
and taste for seasoning.

Heat the oil and butter in a
skillet or frying pan until the
butter foams and fry the chops
over medium heat for 2–3
minutes on each side until
browned, seasoning on 1 side
after turning them. Drain
chops and arrange on a platter in a circle with the bones
pointing up.

Pile the garnish in the
center, spoon a little sauce
around the edge and serve the
rest separately.

Lamb Chops Alsacienne

8 loin or rib lamb chops
2 tablespoons clarified butter
½ cup (¼ lb) cooked ham,
  coarsely chopped
1 can (4 oz) liver pâté
¼ cup sherry
¼ cup stock
8 small mushrooms
2 tablespoons butter
10–12 small new potatoes,
  boiled and tossed in butter
  and chopped parsley (for
  garnish)

For sauce
1 small onion, finely chopped
½ cup white wine
1½ cups Espagnole sauce (see
  Volume 2)
1 teaspoon Dijon-style mustard
2 gherkin pickles, chopped
1 tablespoon chopped parsley
½ teaspoon lemon juice or
  vinegar (optional)

The ham and pâté used in this

recipe are characteristic ingredients of the province of
Alsace, France.

Method
Set oven at hot (400°F).

Trim the fat and meat from
the ends of the chops to
expose about 1 inch of bone;
scrape the bone ends clean.
Flatten chops slightly with a
mallet. In a skillet or frying
pan heat the clarified butter
and fry the chops gently for
2–3 minutes until brown on
1 side only. Take them out
and let cool.

Mix the ham with the pâté
and spread on top of the
browned side of the chops.
Replace the chops carefully in
the pan, uncooked side down,
and fry gently for 2–3 minutes. Pour in the sherry and
stock, cover and transfer to
heated oven and bake for
6–7 minutes.

Sauté the mushrooms in
1 tablespoon butter until
tender and keep warm.

To make the sauce: fry the
onion in the remaining 1
tablespoon butter until
golden brown. Add the wine
and boil until reduced by half.
Add this mixture to the
Espagnole sauce and simmer
8–10 minutes or until glossy
and the consistency of light
cream. Stir in the mustard,
gherkin pickles and parsley,
sharpen the flavor of the
sauce with lemon juice or
vinegar, if you like, and keep
hot without boiling.

Arrange the chops on a
platter, set a mushroom on
top of each and spoon over a
little sauce, serving the rest
separately.

Garnish the platter with
buttered new potatoes and
serve with cabbage Alsacienne.

Cabbage Alsacienne

firm head of cabbage, shredded
1 tablespoon butter
small bunch of celery, finely
  chopped
½ cup dry white wine, or same
  quantity of stock with 2
  teaspoons wine vinegar
salt and pepper
1 tablespoon chopped parsley

Method
Blanch cabbage in pan of boiling salted water for 1 minute,
then drain well.

Melt butter in a shallow pan
or flameproof casserole, add
celery and cook for 2–3 minutes until soft but not brown.
Add the cabbage and wine, or
stock and wine vinegar. Season well; cover and cook
gently for 25–30 minutes.
Sprinkle with chopped parsley
before serving.

Lamb chops Reform – the dish was created by the famous chef Alexis Soyer

Lamb Chops with Herbs

8 loin or rib lamb chops
2 tablespoons clarified butter

For herb stuffing
1 tablespoon chopped parsley
1 teaspoon thyme
$\frac{1}{2}$ teaspoon rosemary
2 shallots, finely chopped
$\frac{1}{4}$ cup butter
1 clove of garlic, crushed
  (optional)
$\frac{3}{4}$ cup fresh white breadcrumbs
salt and pepper

For sauce
1 shallot, finely chopped
4–5 mushrooms, finely
  chopped
$1\frac{1}{2}$ tablespoons flour
2 cups well-flavored stock

*Poultry pins or trussing
  needle and string*

Method
Trim the fat and meat from the ends of the chops to expose about 1 inch of bone, then scrape the bone ends clean. With a small sharp knife cut a pocket in the meat of each chop.

To make herb stuffing: cook the shallots in 2 tablespoons butter until soft but not brown, add the garlic, if used, and cook $\frac{1}{2}$ minute longer. Melt the remaining 2 tablespoons butter in the pan and stir the mixture into the breadcrumbs with the herbs and plenty of seasoning. Put stuffing into the chops and fasten with poultry pins or sew with trussing needle and string.

Heat the clarified butter in a skillet and fry the chops for 2–3 minutes on each side or until golden brown. Transfer them to a baking dish and cook in a low oven (300°F) for 10 minutes.

To make the sauce: add the shallot to the skillet and cook until soft. Stir in the mushrooms with seasoning and cook until all the moisture is evaporated. Add the flour, pour in the stock and bring to a boil, stirring. Simmer the sauce 5–6 minutes or until well flavored and the consistency of light cream; taste for seasoning.

Remove the poultry pins or strings; arrange chops, overlapping, on a platter. Spoon a little sauce over and serve the rest separately. Buttered carrots are a good accompaniment.

Lamb Chops Soubise

8 rib or loin lamb chops
1 onion, sliced
1 carrot, sliced
bouquet garni
$\frac{1}{2}$ cup white wine
$\frac{1}{4}$ cup stock
salt and pepper

For soubise sauce
3 large onions, sliced
5 tablespoons butter
3 tablespoons flour
$1\frac{1}{2}$ cups milk
2 tablespoons heavy cream

To finish
mashed potatoes made with
  4 medium boiled potatoes,
  3–4 tablespoons butter,
  $\frac{1}{2}$ cup hot milk
fried onion rings (see right)

Method
Trim fat and meat from the ends of the chops to expose about 1 inch of the bone, then scrape the bone ends clean. Put the sliced onion and carrot with the bouquet garni in a shallow flameproof casserole, set the chops on top, pour over the wine and stock and season lightly. Cover the pot with foil and the lid and simmer gently for 20–30 minutes or until the chops are very tender.

Make the mashed potatoes and keep warm.

To make the soubise sauce: blanch the large sliced onions and drain them. In a pan melt 2 tablespoons butter, add the onions, press a piece of buttered paper on top, add the lid and cook very gently for 15 minutes or until the onions are very tender but not brown. Work them through a sieve or purée them in a blender. In a saucepan melt the remaining butter, stir in the flour off the heat and pour in the milk. Bring to a boil, stirring, season and simmer 2 minutes.

Strain the liquid from the lamb chops, leaving them in the pan. Skim off any fat and add $\frac{3}{4}$ cup liquid with the onion purée to the sauce. Bring to a boil, simmer 2–3 minutes, stir in the cream and taste for seasoning.

Arrange the mashed potatoes down the center of a platter and set the chops, overlapping, on top. Coat with the soubise sauce and garnish with the fried onion rings.

Push out the onion rings to make the garnish for lamb chops soubise

Fried Onion Rings

Peel 1–2 large Bermuda or Spanish onions, cut them into $\frac{1}{4}$ inch slices and separate them into rings. Barely cover them with milk, let soak 5 minutes, then drain.

Dip the rings first in 1 egg, beaten to mix, and then in seasoned flour. Fry them a few at a time in hot deep fat (375°F on a fat thermometer) until they are crisp and golden. Drain them thoroughly on crumpled paper towels and serve at once.

Côtelettes d'Agneau Volnay
(Lamb Chops Volnay)

8 loin or rib lamb chops
2 tablespoons seasoned flour
  (made with pinch of salt and
  pepper)
1 small egg, beaten to mix
$\frac{1}{4}$ cup finely chopped cooked
  ham
$\frac{1}{4}$ cup fresh white breadcrumbs
2 tablespoons oil
2 tablespoons butter
1 tablespoon chopped parsley
  (for garnish)

For salpicon
$1\frac{1}{2}$ tablespoons butter
1 medium onion, thinly sliced
3–4 medium potatoes, peeled
  and sliced
salt and pepper
$\frac{3}{4}$–1 cup stock
1 cup ($\frac{1}{4}$ lb) mushrooms, sliced

Method
Trim fat and meat from bones of chops to expose 1 inch of bone; scrape bone ends clean.

Coat chops with seasoned flour, brush them with beaten egg and roll them in the ham, mixed with the breadcrumbs, pressing the mixture on well with a spatula.

To make the salpicon: in a skillet melt the butter, add the onion, cover and cook gently until soft but not browned. Add the sliced potatoes with seasoning and $\frac{3}{4}$ cup stock. Cover and simmer 8–10 minutes. Add the sliced mushrooms, press a piece of foil on top, add the lid and cook 4–5 minutes longer until potatoes and mushrooms are tender. The potatoes should absorb all the stock during cooking, but if the mixture gets dry, add a little more stock.

In a large heavy skillet heat the oil and butter and, when foaming, add the chops. Fry the chops over high heat 2–3 minutes on each side or until browned; season them after turning.

Arrange the chops on a platter, bones slanting up, and spoon the salpicon down the other side of the dish. Sprinkle with chopped parsley and serve.

Tournedos Mâconnaise

4 tournedos steaks, cut 1–1$\frac{1}{2}$ inches thick
4 slices of bread, crusts removed (for croûtes)
6 tablespoons oil and butter, mixed (for frying)
salt and pepper

For sauce and garnish
1 cup red wine (Mâcon)
2 tablespoons butter
4 large flat mushrooms, stems trimmed level with caps
2 shallots, finely chopped
2 teaspoons flour
$\frac{1}{2}$ cup well-flavored beef stock
1 teaspoon tomato paste

Method
Boil the wine until it is reduced by about one-third and reserve.

Trim the bread for croûtes the same size as the tournedos. In a heavy skillet heat half the oil and butter, fry the croûtes until golden brown on both sides and drain on paper towels.

Wipe out the pan, heat the remaining oil and butter and fry the tournedos briskly for 2–3 minutes on each side for rare meat, sprinkling with seasoning after turning them. Set them on a platter on top of the croûtes and keep warm.

To make sauce and garnish: add 1$\frac{1}{2}$ tablespoons butter to the pan and sauté the mushrooms gently on each side until tender. Place 1 on top of each tournedos. Add the remaining butter to the pan and cook the shallot gently until soft. Stir in the flour off the heat, pour in the reduced wine with the stock, bring to a boil and simmer 2–3 minutes. Taste the sauce for seasoning.

Spoon sauce and garnish over the tournedos and serve with petits pois à la Française.

Petits Pois à la Française

3–4 cups shelled fresh peas
1 romaine lettuce, shredded
10–12 scallions, cut in 2 inch pieces
2 teaspoons sugar
bouquet garni
$\frac{1}{4}$ cup butter
$\frac{1}{2}$ cup cold water
salt

Another version of this recipe using frozen peas was given in Volume 1.

Method
Put the peas in a saucepan with the lettuce, scallions, sugar, bouquet garni and half the butter; add the water. Cover the pan with a heatproof plate, half-filled with cold water, and cook quickly for 20–25 minutes or until peas and scallions are tender. **Watchpoint:** cold water on top of the pan condenses the steam as it rises and keeps the peas moist during cooking. Add more cold water as the water in the plate evaporates.

Just before serving, remove the bouquet garni and add the remaining butter with salt to taste. Shake pan well to mix and serve peas in hot dish.

Add the scallion pieces to peas and shredded lettuce for petits pois à la Française

Tournedos Seville

4 tournedos steaks, cut 1–1½ inches thick
4 slices of white bread, crusts removed (for croûtes)
4 tablespoons oil and butter, mixed (for frying)
¼ cup sherry

For garnish
1 cup quantity pie pastry (made with 1 cup flour, 3 tablespoons butter, 3 tablespoons shortening, ¼ teaspoon salt and 2–3 tablespoons cold water)
4 cooked artichoke bottoms, fresh, frozen or canned
béchamel sauce, made with 1 tablespoon butter, 1 tablespoon flour, ¾ cup milk (infused with slice of onion, 6 peppercorns, blade of mace and bay leaf)
1 tablespoon heavy cream
salt and pepper
1 tablespoon grated Parmesan cheese

For savory butter
3 tablespoons butter
½ clove of garlic, crushed
1 tablespoon chopped parsley
salt
black pepper, freshly ground

4 deep tartlet pans

Method
Make pie pastry dough and chill 30 minutes. Set the oven at hot (400°F). Roll out dough, line the tartlet pans and prick well; line dough with foil or wax paper and beans and bake blind in heated oven for 10–12 minutes or until golden brown. Let cool in the pans, then remove the pastry shells.

To make the savory butter: cream the butter, work in the garlic, parsley and salt and pepper to taste. Shape into a block on a piece of wax paper,

chill until firm and cut in 4 equal pieces.

To prepare garnish: prepare fresh artichoke bottoms or drain canned ones, or cook frozen ones according to package directions. Make the béchamel sauce, cover and keep warm.

Cut the croûtes the same size as the tournedos and fry in half the oil and butter until golden brown on both sides; drain on paper towels.

Place the artichoke bottoms in the pastry cases. Reheat the béchamel sauce, add the cream, taste for seasoning and spoon over the artichoke hearts. Sprinkle with Parmesan cheese and bake in heated oven for about 5 minutes or until browned.

In a heavy skillet heat the remaining oil and butter and briskly fry the tournedos for 2–3 minutes on each side for rare steak; sprinkle with seasoning after turning them. Place each tournedos on a croûte, arrange on a platter, set the tartlet cases between them and keep warm.

Add the sherry to the skillet and simmer to dissolve the pan juices. Cook until reduced by about one-third; spoon over the tournedos. Place a pat of savory butter on each tournedos and serve at once.

Escalopes Savoyarde

4 large veal escalopes (about 1½ lb)
¼ cup butter (for frying)
salt and pepper
¼ cup dry vermouth
1 medium onion, finely chopped
4 slices of cooked ham
béchamel sauce, made with 1½ tablespoons butter, 1 tablespoon flour, 1 cup milk (infused with slice of onion, 6 peppercorns, blade of mace and bay leaf)
3 tablespoons heavy cream
½ cup grated Gruyère cheese

For garnish
1 lb fresh green beans, trimmed
1 tablespoon butter

Method
In a large skillet heat 3 tablespoons of the butter until foaming and sauté the escalopes for 2–3 minutes on each side until brown; sprinkle with seasoning after turning them. Add the vermouth, simmer until reduced a little, arrange the veal flat in a baking dish and spoon over the pan juices.

Melt the remaining butter in the pan, cook the onion until lightly browned and scatter it over the escalopes.

Cover each escalope with a slice of ham. Set the oven at moderately hot (375°F).

Make the béchamel sauce, add the cream and bring just back to a boil. Take from the heat, stir in half the cheese and taste for seasoning. Coat the escalopes with sauce, sprinkle with the remaining cheese and bake in heated oven for 10–15 minutes or until browned.

To prepare garnish: cook the green beans in boiling salted water for 12–15 minutes until tender; drain, refresh and drain again.

Reheat the beans in the butter.

Transfer the escalopes to a serving dish and spoon green beans down each side.

Veal Chops Monarque

4 loin or rib veal chops
¼ cup clarified butter
1 cup (¼ lb) mushrooms, finely chopped
½ cup grated Gruyère cheese
salt
black pepper, freshly ground
½ cup stock
½ package (½ lb) conchiglie (small pasta shells)
1 tablespoon butter
2 slices of cooked ham, cut in strips
¼ cup port

Method
Set the oven at hot (400°F).

In a skillet or shallow flame-proof casserole heat 2 tablespoons clarified butter and fry the chops slowly on 1 side only until golden brown; take from the pan. Add the mushrooms and cook over high heat until all the moisture is evaporated. Take from heat and stir in the cheese.

Season to taste and spread this mixture on the browned side of the chops.

Melt the remaining clarified butter in the pan, replace the chops and brown the uncooked sides for 2–3 minutes. Pour in the stock and cover; transfer pan to heated oven and bake the chops for 15–20 minutes or until they are tender.

Cook the conchiglie in plenty of simmering salted water for the time stated on the package or until almost tender ('al dente'). Drain them, rinse with cold water and reheat them with 1 tablespoon butter, the strips of ham and plenty of pepper, tossing to mix well.

Take out the chops, arrange in a serving dish and keep warm. Add the port to the pan and bring to a boil, stirring to dissolve the pan juices. Boil until well reduced.

Strain the sauce over the chops and garnish the platter with the ham and conchiglie.

◀ *Spread cooked mushroom and cheese mixture on the browned side of the veal chops*

Veal chops Monarque are garnished with the ham and conchiglie mixture

Hungarian grenadins of veal are garnished with triangular croûtes dipped in parsley

Grenadins de Veau à l'Hongroise
(Hungarian Grenadins of Veal)

8 veal grenadins
1 medium eggplant
mornay sauce (made with
 $2\frac{1}{2}$ tablespoons butter,
 $2\frac{1}{2}$ tablespoons flour,
 $1\frac{1}{2}$ cups milk, 6 tablespoons
 grated Parmesan or Gruyère
 cheese and $\frac{3}{4}$ teaspoon
 Dijon-style mustard)
$\frac{1}{4}$ cup seasoned flour (made
 with $\frac{1}{4}$ teaspoon salt and
 pinch of pepper)
4–5 tablespoons clarified butter
1 shallot, finely chopped
1 teaspoon paprika
$\frac{1}{4}$ cup white wine
1 cup heavy cream
salt and pepper
1 tablespoon grated Parmesan
 cheese

For Garnish
2–3 slices of bread, crusts
 removed, cut in triangles and
 fried in 2–3 tablespoons oil
 and butter (mixed) with tips
 dipped in chopped parsley
 (for croûtes)

Method
Cut the eggplant into $\frac{1}{2}$ inch slices, score them lightly with a knife, sprinkle with salt, cover and let stand 30 minutes to draw out the juices (dégorger). Make the mornay sauce and keep covered.

Rinse the eggplant slices, pat dry with paper towels and sprinkle with half the seasoned flour.

Melt 2 tablespoons clarified butter in a skillet and fry the eggplant slices over medium heat for 2–3 minutes on each side or until brown and tender, adding more clarified butter during cooking, if necessary; reserve them.

Coat the grenadins with the remaining seasoned flour and fry them gently in the remaining butter for 4–5 minutes on each side or until golden brown. Arrange in a heatproof serving dish or gratin dish, set a slice of eggplant on top of each grenadin and keep warm.

Add the shallot to the pan and cook gently for 2 minutes or until soft. Add the paprika and cook 2 minutes longer. Pour on the wine and boil until reduced by half. Stir in the cream, bring the sauce just to a boil, taste for seasoning and keep warm.

Reheat the mornay sauce without boiling, spoon it over the grenadins and sprinkle them with the grated cheese. Brown them under the broiler or in a hot oven (400°F), spoon the paprika sauce around the dish and garnish with croûtes.

A **grenadin** is a small piece of veal, resembling a tournedos steak, cut $\frac{1}{2}$–$\frac{3}{4}$ inch thick and usually taken from the round. Two grenadins weigh about $\frac{1}{3}$ lb and serve 1 person.

Chicken with Almonds

$3\frac{1}{2}$–4 lb roasting chicken
2 carrots, sliced
1 onion, sliced
bouquet garni
6 peppercorns
salt

For sauce
2 tablespoons butter
2 tablespoons flour
$1\frac{1}{2}$–2 cups chicken stock
 (see method)
2 tablespoons heavy cream

For garnish
2 tablespoons butter
2 onions, sliced
$\frac{1}{3}$ cup slivered almonds
juice of $\frac{1}{2}$ lemon
pepper

Method
Put the chicken in a kettle with the carrots, onion, bouquet garni, peppercorns, a little salt and water to cover. Cover the pan and poach the chicken for 35 minutes or until almost tender. Take out, cut it in pieces and lay them in a small roasting pan or shallow casserole. Boil the stock to reduce it to $1\frac{1}{2}$–2 cups.

To prepare garnish: in a skillet melt 1 tablespoon butter and fry the onions until golden brown. Take them out, melt the remaining butter and fry the almonds until browned also. Take from the heat, stir in the onions and lemon juice with seasoning and spoon the mixture over chicken pieces. Sprinkle them with 1–2 tablespoons chicken stock and bake in a moderate oven (350°F) for 20 minutes or until they are very tender.

To make the sauce: in a pan melt the butter, stir in the flour and cook until straw-colored. Pour in the chicken stock, bring to a boil, stirring, and simmer 5–6 minutes or until the sauce is the consistency of heavy cream. Add the cream and taste for seasoning.

Transfer chicken pieces to a platter or leave in the casserole, spoon a little sauce around the dish and serve the rest separately.

After beef has set in aspic, garnish it with diamonds of truffle and cover with aspic (recipe is on page 56)

ENRICH BEEF FILLET WITH PATE AND TRUFFLES

For a luxurious menu try cold fillet of beef, enriched with pâté and truffles and glistening with golden aspic or for a hot entrée, braise beef with Champagne. Add fresh asparagus soup, and a ripe melon filled with fruits and served with homemade petits fours for elegance that makes a menu easy to prepare ahead.

The handsome beef dish requires an equally stylish wine. The best reds of Volnay, in Burgundy's Côte de Beaune district, can be just that — full of flavor but rather light on the palate. A good domestic alternative would be a Pinot Noir from California's Santa Clara valley. With the dessert of melon and its accompanying petits fours, another light wine seems appropriate — this time white with a touch of sweetness. Try a Riesling from Alsace or California's Grey Riesling.

Cream of Asparagus Soup
Melba Toast

Médaillons de Boeuf en Gelée
(Sliced Beef in Aspic)

Vichy Salad
or

Boeuf Braisé au Champagne
(Braised Beef with Champagne)
Morels with Cream

Melon en Surprise with Petits Fours

Red wine — Volnay (Côte de Beaune) or Pinot Noir (California)
White wine — Riesling (Alsace) or Grey Riesling (California)

TIMETABLE

Day before
Make petits fours and store in an airtight container.

Roast fillet of beef, cover and store in refrigerator. *Or braise beef, strain cooking liquid, skim off fat and leave beef and liquid in pot ready for reheating; keep in refrigerator.*

Make aspic; make mayonnaise for Vichy salad and eggs and vinaigrette dressing for potatoes.

Morning
Make asparagus soup but do not add liaison.

Make filling for eggs and keep covered in refrigerator. Keep egg whites in a bowl of cold water.

Peel potatoes and keep in cold water.

Peel carrots and keep in cold water.

Chop parsley for garnish.

Frost cherries, if using, for decorating melon.

Cut melon, discard seeds and fibers; prepare melon balls, remaining cherries and raspberries. Macerate all fruits with sugar and sherry, cover and refrigerate. Tie melon shell in plastic bag before refrigerating.

Arrange beef and topping in shallow dish or tray, coat with aspic, garnish with truffle or mushrooms and finish with more aspic. Keep in refrigerator.

Make morels in cream but do not add sour cream; keep in refrigerator. Cook, shape and coat potato croquettes, but do not fry; keep covered.

Assemble ingredients for final cooking from 6:45 for dinner around 8 p.m.

Order of Work
6:45
Set oven at moderate (350°F) to reheat braised beef.
7:00
Put braised beef in oven.
7:15
Boil potatoes. Cut out médaillons of beef and arrange on serving platter. Chop remaining aspic and add to platter.
7:30
Drain potatoes and toss in vinaigrette dressing while still warm. Keep at room temperature. *Or fry potato croquettes and keep warm in a low oven (300°F) with door open. Reheat morels gently on top of stove.*

Drain carrots and cut in julienne strips. Mix mayonnaise with remaining ingredients; finish salad and keep in serving dish at room temperature.
7:45
Arrange petits fours in serving dish. Fill melon with macerated fruits and add lid, or garnish with frosted cherries, and place on decorative leaves.

Transfer braised beef to a platter and keep warm. Make sauce.

Reheat asparagus soup, add liaison and garnish.

Add sour cream to morels and transfer to a serving dish.
8:00
Serve appetizer.

Arrange potatoes in center of médaillons of beef platter and sprinkle with parsley just before serving.

Appetizer
Cream of Asparagus Soup

1 lb fresh asparagus
4 cups veal or chicken stock
1 small onion, finely chopped
2 tablespoons butter
1½ tablespoons flour
salt and pepper
Melba toast (for serving)

For liaison
2 egg yolks
6 tablespoons heavy cream

Method
Trim the white part from the asparagus stalks, then rinse them in cold water and with a vegetable peeler remove the tough skin from the lower ends of the stalks. Cut into 1 inch pieces and put them in a pan with the stock and onion. Cover the pan, bring to a boil and simmer 6–8 minutes or until the asparagus is tender. Reserve a few tips for garnish. Work asparagus and liquid through a nylon sieve or purée in a blender.

Melt the butter in a large pan, stir in flour and cook, stirring, until straw-colored. Take from heat and add the asparagus purée. Season and bring the soup to a boil, stirring, and simmer 2–3 minutes.

Mix the egg yolks and cream together and add a little of the hot soup before adding this liaison to remaining soup. Reheat carefully without boiling, adjust seasoning, add reserved asparagus tips and serve with Melba toast separately.

Melba Toast

Toast slices of white bread, and trim the crusts. Hold the toast flat on a board with your hand and, with a sharp knife, carefully slice between the toasted sides to make two thin slices. Bake the split slices in a moderate oven (350°F) until the untoasted sides are lightly brown and the toast is very crisp. Store in an airtight container if not for immediate use.

Hold the slice of toast flat with one hand and carefully slice it horizontally with a sharp knife. This makes two very thin slices that are toasted on one side only

You will find that **cooking times** given in the individual recipes for these dishes have sometimes been adapted in the timetable to help you when cooking and serving this menu as a party meal.

Good melba toast is lightly browned and very crisp

Entrée

Médaillons de Boeuf en Gelée
(Sliced Beef in Aspic)

2 lb piece of beef fillet
2 tablespoons oil
1 canned truffle, drained, or
　6–8 small mushrooms
squeeze of lemon juice
　(optional)
6 tablespoons butter, creamed
2 cans (4 oz each) pâté de foie
¼ teaspoon Dijon-style mustard
　(optional)
2 teaspoons sherry (optional)
½ lb thinly sliced cooked ham
　or Canadian bacon
4 cups cool but still liquid
　aspic (see Volume 8)

*4–5 inch oval or round cookie
cutter (optional)*

Method
To roast the fillet of beef: heat the oil in a roasting pan, baste the beef and roast in a hot oven (400°F) for 40 minutes or until a meat thermometer inserted in the center registers 140°F for rare beef. Let the beef stand at room temperature until cold.

If using a truffle, thinly slice it and cut slices in diamonds; chop and reserve the trimmings. If using mushrooms, trim the stems level with the caps and cook the caps, covered, in a small pan with 1–2 tablespoons water and a squeeze of lemon juice for 2 minutes or until the mushrooms are just tender. Drain them.

Work the creamed butter into the pâté and, if using truffle, beat in the chopped truffle trimmings. If using mushrooms, add the mustard and sherry to the pâté.

Carve the cold fillet into ½ inch slices. Trim a piece of ham to the same size as each slice of beef. Spread a layer of pâté mixture on each piece of beef and arrange a slice of ham on top; press together lightly and smooth the edges. Lay the slices (they should be about ¾ inch thick) in a shallow dish or tray and spoon in just enough cool but still liquid aspic to cover. Chill until the aspic is firm, then garnish each beef slice with a diamond or truffle or a whole cooked mushroom.

Add another layer of cool aspic to cover the garnish and chill until very firm.

To serve, using a round or oval cutter or knife, cut around each arrangement of beef to make médaillons and place on a serving platter. Chop the remaining aspic and place around the meat. Serve with boiled small potatoes, mixed with vinaigrette dressing and sprinkled with chopped parsley, and Vichy salad (recipe is on page 84).

Set the truffle garnish for médaillons de boeuf in aspic

Truffles

Much prized by gourmets for their unique flavor, truffles are a rather mysterious food. They are coal-black fungi, sometimes as large as apples, that grow underground attached to the roots of stunted oak trees.

The truffles with the most delicious flavor and aroma come from the Périgord region of France. Less good black truffles grow elsewhere in southern France, Italy and North Africa. White truffles, with a slightly peppery flavor, are found in Piedmont, Italy.

Truffles can be harvested only once a year after the first frosts of fall. Many attempts have been made to cultivate them but without success; the only way to find them is to use dogs or pigs trained to sniff them out. Truffle hunting and packaging is one of the chief rural industries in Périgord.

Truffles are available here in cans but they are expensive. In a can there may be 1 large truffle or several irregularly-shaped smaller ones. Canned truffle pieces are also sold and they are cheaper. Any small pieces that are trimmed off when shaping a truffle for slicing may be used to flavor pâté — as in our recipe for sliced beef in aspic — or added to stuffings.

Alternative entrée

Boeuf Braisé au Champagne
(Braised Beef with Champagne)

5 lb beef rib roast
2 teaspoons arrowroot, mixed
　to a paste with 2 tablespoons
　water

For braising
1 bottle of Champagne
1 calf's foot, split
2 tablespoons oil
2 onions, sliced
2 carrots, sliced
2 cups beef stock
bouquet garni
salt and pepper

Method
Wash the split calf's foot thoroughly, blanch it in boiling water for 5 minutes, and drain.

In a large flameproof casserole heat the oil and brown the beef on both flat sides. Add the calf's foot and about three-quarters of the Champagne, cover and braise in a moderately low oven (325°F) for 30 minutes.

Add the onions and carrots, 1 cup stock, bouquet garni and seasoning. Lower the oven temperature to 300°F and cook 2–3 hours longer or until the beef is very tender. When the liquid evaporates during cooking add the remaining Champagne and stock. Transfer the beef to a platter and keep warm.

Discard the calf's foot and strain the cooking liquid, pressing the vegetables well to extract all the juice. Skim off the fat and, if necessary, boil to reduce to 2 cups. Stir in the arrowroot paste and bring the sauce just back to a boil, stirring until it thickens. Taste for seasoning, spoon a little sauce over the beef and serve the rest separately.

Garnish the platter with potato croquettes and serve morels in cream separately, if you like.

Accompaniment to alternative entrée

Potato Croquettes

Cook 5 medium potatoes in boiling salted water for 15 minutes or until tender. Drain. Work them through a strainer or ricer and return them to the pan; beat in 2 tablespoons butter, 2 egg yolks, $\frac{1}{4}$ cup hot milk, salt and pepper.

Cool the potato mixture, roll it out onto a floured board into a 1-inch thick cylinder. Cut into 2-inch lengths. Roll the croquettes in flour, seasoned with salt and pepper, and brush them with 1 egg, beaten to mix with $\frac{1}{2}$ teaspoon salt.

Coat the potato croquettes with dry white breadcrumbs. Fry them in butter, turning them so they brown evenly, or fry them in hot deep fat (375°F on a fat thermometer) until golden brown. Drain well on paper towels.

Morels with Cream

1 cup dried or 1 can (12 oz) morel mushrooms
2 tablespoons butter
1 tablespoon flour
1 cup heavy cream
salt and pepper
$\frac{1}{4}$ teaspoon nutmeg
$\frac{1}{3}$ cup sour cream

Button mushrooms may be substituted for morels in this recipe. Use 1 lb small mushrooms and trim the stems. Sauté them in butter and continue cooking as for morels.

Method
Soak dried morels in warm water to cover for 30 minutes and drain, or drain canned morels. Dry them on paper towels.

Heat the butter, add the morels and sauté 2 minutes. Stir in the flour, add the heavy cream and bring to a boil, stirring. Season with salt, pepper and nutmeg and simmer 2 minutes or until the sauce is fairly thick.

Just before serving, stir in the sour cream and reheat without boiling.

Morels are considered the second favorite fungus to truffles. They are dark and wrinkled with a rich aromatic flavor. Morels grow wild in a few areas of the U.S. and are available dried or in cans.

Dessert

Melon en Surprise

1 Crenshaw, Casaba or honeydew melon
$\frac{1}{2}$ lb fresh Bing cherries
1 pint fresh raspberries or 1 package frozen raspberries, thawed and drained
3–4 tablespoons sugar
$\frac{1}{4}$ cup sherry

To finish (optional)
few frosted cherries
$\frac{1}{2}$ egg white
granulated sugar (for coating)

Method
Cut the top off the melon, carefully scoop out and discard the seeds and fibers. Remove the melon flesh in balls with a ball cutter. Pit the cherries, reserving a few with their stems to frost for decoration, if you like. Pick over the raspberries if fresh. Put the cherries, raspberries and melon balls in a bowl, sprinkle over the sugar and sherry, cover tightly and leave to macerate in the refrigerator for 1–2 hours. Tie the melon shell in a plastic bag and chill. **Watchpoint:** it is important to cover the melon when chilling in the refrigerator since its penetrating odor and flavor will be absorbed by any other uncovered food.

To serve melon, remove the chilled fruit from the refrigerator, pile it back into the melon shell and replace the top of the melon as a lid. Alternatively, top the fruit with frosted cherries.

Set the melon on a dessert platter lined with vine leaves or any decorative leaves. Serve with a selection of petits

fours, such as macarons à l'orange and muscadins (recipes are on next page).

To Frost Cherries

Pit the cherries but leave on the stems. Brush cherries lightly with $\frac{1}{2}$ an egg white, beaten until frothy, roll them in granulated sugar to coat well and let dry on a wire rack.

Cut the top off the melon, discard the seeds and fibers and scoop out the flesh in balls with a ball cutter

Accompaniments to dessert

Petits Fours
Basic Mixture

1 cup whole blanched almonds,
  ground
2 tablespoons flour
½ cup sugar
4 egg whites

Method
Mix the almonds, flour and sugar together and work through a coarse strainer to make sure they are evenly mixed. Stiffly beat egg whites and fold into the almond mixture. Use as directed in the recipes given here.

Note: recipes for petits fours on the right are each made from half the quantity of the basic mixture, with other ingredients as specified.

Any of the recipes given in the lesson on **petits fours** in Volume 16 would be equally suitable to serve with this melon en surprise; also the **columbines, minerves** or **Suédoises** recipes given in Volume 18.

Macarons à l'Orange
(Small Orange Macaroons)

½ quantity of basic mixture
1½ tablespoons orange liqueur
  such as Curaçao, Triple Sec
  or Grand Marnier, or grated
  rind and strained juice of
  ½ orange
1 cup confectioners' sugar
1 tablespoon apricot jam

Pastry bag; ¼ inch plain tube

Makes 6–8 macaroons.

Method
Set the oven at moderate (350°F) and line a baking sheet with silicone paper.

Flavor the basic mixture with half the chosen liqueur or grated orange rind. Put the mixture into the pastry bag fitted with the plain tube and pipe in tiny rounds onto the prepared baking sheet. Bake in heated oven for 6–7 minutes or until lightly browned. Cool macaroons on a wire rack.

Mix the confectioners' sugar to a fairly thick paste with remaining liqueur or a little strained orange juice to make orange icing. Add 1–2 teaspoons water, if necessary. Sandwich the flat sides of 2 macaroons together with a little apricot jam. Warm the orange icing carefully to tepid in a small double boiler or over a pan of hot water — it should coat the back of a spoon. Spear the sandwiched macaroons carefully with a 2-pronged fork and dip them in the icing or spoon a little icing over the top of the macaroons to coat them.

Muscadins

½ quantity of basic mixture
2–3 tablespoons praline
  powder
2 squares (2 oz) semisweet
  chocolate, chopped
½ teaspoon oil

Pastry bag; ¼ inch plain tube

Makes 6–8 muscadins.

Method
Put the basic mixture in the pastry bag fitted with the plain tube, pipe into rounds and bake in the same way as for the orange macaroons, but do not add any liqueur or orange rind. After baking, while the muscadins are still warm and soft, hollow the base of each with your finger. Pound the praline powder to a paste.

Watchpoint: this pounding is easiest done with a small wooden pestle but it can be done with the end of a rolling pin. The pounding releases the almond oil and binds the praline.

Fill the hollows of the muscadins with praline paste and sandwich them together. Melt the chocolate with the oil in a pan of hot water, but do not let it get more than tepid or the icing will be dull. Spear the muscadins with a 2-pronged fork, dip them in the chocolate or spoon the chocolate over them to coat completely, and set them aside to dry in a cool place.

Praline Powder
For about ¼ cup: put ¼ cup unblanched almonds and ¼ cup sugar in a small heavy-based pan. Cook over low heat until the sugar melts, shaking pan occasionally. When the sugar turns a pale golden brown, stir mixture with a metal spoon and continue cooking until it is dark brown, but do not let it burn. Pour at once onto an oiled baking sheet and leave until cold and hard. Grind in a rotary cheese grater or a grinder or work in a blender a little at a time.

Praline powder can be stored in an airtight container — it may become soft and sticky, but the flavor will not be impaired.

A luxury menu

Melon en surprise is served with macarons à l'orange and muscadins petits fours

59

Winter melon soup (recipe is on page 65)

CHINESE COOKING

Color, texture and taste are combined in perfect balance in Chinese cooking. The essential characteristics of food are carefully studied so that in any dish, the flavor of each ingredient is heightened while at the same time blending with the others, so no one single flavor — salty, bland, sweet, sour, bitter, hot, fragrant or golden—is dominant. It is the only style of cooking that rivals French cuisine in its scope and subtlety and many connoisseurs claim that Chinese cooking is superior.

As in France, dishes and styles of Chinese cooking vary from region to region. Here the best known Chinese cooking is Cantonese because the first Chinese to come to the U.S. in the 19th century were from Canton. Even now, most of the Chinese population here is of Cantonese descent. This feature covers Cantonese cooking only.

Subtle blending of flavor, exact attention to timing — particularly of vegetables — and quick cooking are characteristic of all Chinese dishes but especially those from Canton. Less oil is used than in other areas and common ingredients include nuts, mushrooms, seafood, pork and poultry. The guiding principle in Cantonese steam cooking is 'Ching', meaning clear or simple and green; starchy, wheat-based foods like noodles are used less than in northern provinces.

Preparation is enormously important and often accounts for nearly all of the time spent in making a Chinese dish. All necessary chopping and cutting is done in the kitchen because the Chinese regard knives as weapons and will therefore never place them on the table. Vegetables are meticulously sliced, cubed or cut in chunks, strips, curls, fans or flowers of even size so that finished dishes have a pleasing symmetry. Meats and poultry are also always cut up either before or after cooking so they are bite-size and can be eaten with chopsticks. However, fish is often served whole.

Methods of cooking can be simple like 'stir-frying' (toss-cooking), where the ingredients of a dish are quickly cooked in oil over high heat until lightly cooked, usually without browning; steaming and poaching are other common cooking processes, particularly in Canton; roasting or barbecuing and deep frying are also popular.

The late **John J. Kan,** author of this feature, was a pioneer in introducing the art of Chinese cooking to Americans. He inherited his cooking talents from his mother and was always closely associated with food. Founder of the well-known Kan's Restaurant in San Francisco's Chinatown, Johnny Kan was the first to print a dictionary menu for his customers. Over 25 years ago, he introduced that indispensable Chinese cooking utensil, the **wok,** to American cooks. The recipes in this feature are from his book 'Eight Immortal Flavors' published by Howell-North Books, Berkeley, Cal.

Choosing Menus

Chinese menus are selected with just as much care as the ingredients of the individual dishes. In general there are 3 styles of dining in China — **village** or **simple,** the more elaborate **dinner**-style, and the full **banquet.**

A village-style menu will include homey dishes like bean cake sautéed with meat, Chinese chard with oil and salt, and steamed eggs with clams.

The more elaborate dinner-style menu may feature more sophisticated dishes like dry fried shrimps in shell, oyster sauce beef, and snow peas sautéed with water chestnuts and bamboo shoots.

Recipes in this feature suitable for a banquet are winter melon soup or shark's fin soup, curried crab in shell, chicken à la Kan, lotus stuffed duck, fresh asparagus chicken with black bean sauce and lychee pineapple pork sweet and sour.

When serving a village- or dinner-style menu, a soup and 2–3 other dishes besides rice are enough for 2 people. For more people, serve soup, and as many different dishes as there are people plus one extra dish for the table, and rice.

The minimum number for a banquet-style dinner is 8 people; you may serve 1–2 soups, a vegetable or vegetable combination dish, a seafood dish, a meat dish, and 1 or 2 duck, squab or chicken dishes.

Rice is an essential part of less formal Chinese meals and it should be served with all the main dishes of village- and dinner-style menus to act as a foil. At a banquet, rice is never served until the end of the feast because it is considered inappropriate to serve your guests an inexpensive filler.

Tea always accompanies a Chinese meal and there are many different kinds — scented, spicy, light and rich. For the best flavor, make tea in a porcelain pot with rapidly boiling water and for Chinese teas, let it steep 10–15 minutes before drinking. A heaping teaspoon of tea leaves makes 6 small cups of tea. (This timing does not apply to Orange Pekoe teas as they become bitter if steeped too long.)

On special occasions, the Chinese also drink wine, made from rice or grain. (There are no vineyards in China.) Although there are dozens of wines, the main types are Shooching, a yellow wine, Ng Gah Pay, a dark yellow or amber wine, and Kaoling, similar to vodka but much smoother. Shooching is a favorite in north China. It is warmed and served in delicate porcelain pots, then poured into tiny egg-shell thin cups.

In Cantonese cooking, a simple but potent white wine, commonly called Mai-Jow or rice wine, is found in every home. It is versatile when added sparingly to a dish of quick sautéed vegetables.

Cooking Equipment

With practice and a little improvisation, you can make most Chinese dishes with your regular kitchen equipment. However, a few extra items are particularly helpful.

Wok is the all-purpose Chinese pan. It is particularly designed for stir-frying and it is also used for steaming, stewing, boiling and deep-frying. Shaped like a salad bowl, a wok needs a circle of metal to support it over a regular stove burner. A gas burner is almost essential for using a wok as the curved base of the pan only touches a small area of an electric burner. The traditional wok is made of stainless steel or iron and has a lid — family size measures 14 inches in diameter. A heavy skillet is the best substitute.

Steamer. Many Chinese dishes are steamed — a regular aluminum steamer or large pot is quite adequate or there are special Chinese steamers equipped with bamboo or aluminum trays for stacking so several dishes can be steamed at once.

Chinese cleaver is a splendidly versatile tool and comes in 2 sizes. The large cleaver (dai doh) is used for splitting poultry bones or lobster and crab shells, for chopping spareribs or other meat with small bones or for cubing fish. With the flat side, you can pound steaks and crush ginger or garlic and the thick back of the cleaver is used for mashing ingredients such as scallions.

The small cleaver (choy-doh), almost the same size but lighter in weight, is an all-purpose paring, slicing and chopping knife for vegetables and for shaving paper-thin slices of meat, poultry and fish. The flat of the cleaver makes a handy scoop for finely chopped food and the round wooden handle can be used as a pestle for crushing garlic or beans.

Chopsticks are used for cooking as well as eating. Inexpensive bamboo chopsticks are ideal for stirring, mixing, piercing rice while draining and they even beat egg whites satisfactorily. But for the sophisticated Chinese gourmet, nothing less than genuine ivory chopsticks ($100 or more per pair) are acceptable for the banquet table.

Chicken à la Kan with Virginia ham and broccoli (recipe is on page 72)

Stir-frying

This means to cook very quickly in a little oil over high heat tossing constantly so ingredients retain their fresh flavors and individual textures. The skill in stir-frying lies in perfect timing and even cooking; dishes are quick to make but cannot be kept waiting.

To stir-fry or toss-cook: prepare all the ingredients before you start – it is very important that they should be evenly cut to the exact dimensions given in the recipe so they cook through in the stated time.

In a wok heat oil until a drop of water tossed in sizzles vigorously. Add ingredients in stated recipe order and toss and turn them over constantly, scooping underneath so they blend evenly. The Chinese use a ladle for this and a special turner that looks like a shovel, but 2 large spoons can be substituted.

More ingredients and seasonings may be added while the dish is cooking and often cornstarch is used to thicken the sauce at the end of cooking. When the cornstarch has thickened and the sauce coats ingredients thoroughly, serve the dish at once.

Chinese Ingredients

Chinese grocery stores in cities with Chinatowns carry fresh vegetables and fruits as well as canned, dried and preserved Chinese foods, and many large towns have stores that stock a few basic Chinese products. With these basics, you can make many Chinese dishes using ingredients available in local markets.

The following seasonings are essential:

Black beans, salted, cured and fermented (dow see). You can identify real dow see by its pungent odor and salted appearance. Rinse, mash and store in an airtight container to combine when needed with soy sauce, oil, chopped garlic and a dash of rice wine according to other ingredients in the recipe.

Ginger root (sang geong). Fresh ginger root has a spicy, refreshing quality and is often added to fish and strong meats to reduce the fishy or gamey flavor. Keep roots of ginger in a cool place or peel, finely chop or slice the ginger and store for up to 2 weeks in plastic wrap or an airtight container in the refrigerator until ready to use.

Monosodium glutamate (mei jing) is an additive for heightening flavor. There have been warnings against the effects of MSG, but it has been used in the Orient for decades. Buy a good brand that is 99% pure.

Soy sauce (see yow). Insist on pure, naturally fermented soy sauce; do not accept imitations – they are easily identifiable by reading the fine print that states 'contains caramel coloring, water, salt and protein derivatives'. A lighter soy sauce (sang chau) is also available and it is best used for flavoring or dipping.

Other typically Chinese ingredients called for in these recipes are:

Bamboo shoots (jook soon). Cut from the bamboo bush and canned in chunks, these shoots add crisp texture to soups and stir-fried dishes.

Bean cake (dow foo) or **bean curd** is a smooth custard-like mixture made from puréed soy beans. It comes in 3 inches X $\frac{1}{2}$ inch squares and has a subtle flavor that blends readily with just about any ingredient. It spoils easily, is delicate and needs only reheating, not cooking.

Fermented bean cakes (foo yee) are pressed bean curd cubes that are packed in jars and fermented in alcohol. They are a pungent condiment similar in taste to Liederkranz cheese.

Bean sauce (min see jeong) is a brown, salty paste packed in cans or jars; it is often used with fish and bland vegetables like cauliflower.

Red bean paste (nom yee) is a sweet purée of Chinese red beans. Available in cans, it is used in steamed pastries and sweet dishes.

Bitter melon (foo gwa) looks like a cucumber with a very wrinkled skin. It has a curious sharp and quinine-like refreshing flavor and must always be blanched before using for soups, or for steamed, braised or stir-fried dishes.

Winter melon (doong gwa) is very large and round with a tough green skin and delicate white flesh. It can be sliced to be stir-fried as a vegetable as well as being used for soup.

Kantonese salt (wah yeem) is a spiced seasoning salt often used as a dip for deep-fried poultry.

Chinese chard (bok choy) looks rather like Chinese cabbage. It is a staple vegetable in China, valued more for its texture than for its bland taste.

Chinese dried sausage (lop cheong) is a richly flavored pork sausage that is sold in small links. Cook it by steaming or simmering until the fat is translucent or parboil it to cook further with other meats and vegetables.

Chinese mushrooms (doong goo). Several varieties of Chinese dried mushrooms are available but the type called for here is a dried black mushroom that measures $\frac{1}{2}$–2 inches in diameter and expands when soaked. Its flavor is meaty and rich.

Chinese parsley (yuen sai) is the same as fresh coriander and cilantro. It has a stronger, more aromatic flavor than regular parsley and is used for garnishing as well as flavoring.

Chinese smoked duck liver (opp geok bow) is hard and brown and is wrapped in cured duck's feet. It has an intense, meaty flavor and must be soaked 2 hours or more before chopping to add to steamed dishes.

Dried mandarin orange peel (gaw pay) is the most famous example of the 'gold' element flavoring. This brownish dried peel of the mandarin orange must be soaked for 2 hours until soft; drain before use.

Fuzzy squash (mo gwa) is a green squash covered with a thin, fuzzy skin. It is usually about 4 inches long and is used in soups and stir-fried dishes.

Ginkgo nuts are the thin-shelled seed of a fruit resembling a persimmon. The nut has a sweet, mildly resinous flavor.

Lotus nuts (leen gee) are a symbol of fertility. The ripe nuts are oval with a dark brown husk that must be removed before use; they are also available in cans.

Oils (yow). Chinese cooks like to use vegetable oils, particularly for stir-frying; regular corn and peanut oil are fine.

Oyster sauce (ho yow) literally means essence of oysters. It is thick, brown and rich and used over eggs, as a dip for boiled chicken or roast pork, and for seasoning. A little goes a long way.

Plum sauce (seen mouie jeong) is piquant with a sweet and sour flavor like chutney. It is used for dipping, often with duck.

Snow peas (ho lon dow) or **pea pods** or **sugar peas** are flat, Chinese peas. They are usually 3–4 inches long and used whole or shredded after tips and strings are removed by hand.

Water chestnuts (mah tai) have a dark tough outer skin that should be peeled off before use. This crisp sweet-flavored vegetable is used in a variety of dishes and is also available peeled, whole or sliced, in cans.

Doong Gwa Joong
(Winter Melon Soup)

10 lb Chinese winter melon
$\frac{1}{4}$ cup canned bamboo shoots, drained and sliced
$\frac{1}{2}$ cup (2 oz) button mushrooms
$\frac{1}{4}$ cup washed, dried lotus nuts
$\frac{3}{4}$ cup (6 oz) diced uncooked chicken breast
$1\frac{1}{2}$–2 quarts Chinese chicken stock
$\frac{1}{2}$ cup frozen green peas
salt (to taste)
monosodium glutamate (to taste)
1 inch square dried mandarin peel, softened in cold water, drained and finely chopped

Serves 6 people.

Method
Wash and scrub melon, then cut a 3 inch slice from the top. Scoop out the seeds and discard them; cut the edge of the melon in a zigzag pattern. In the melon cup put the bamboo shoots, mushrooms, lotus nuts and chicken with enough stock to fill melon three-quarters full. Place melon in a deep heatproof dish or pan to support it, then place this dish or pan on a trivet or rack inside a large kettle – this kettle must be wide enough so the melon and its supporting dish or pan can be easily lifted in and out. Add 3–4 inches water to the kettle, then cover and steam for about 1–2 hours if using a young melon, or 3–4 hours if using an old one, or until the flesh is tender. Add hot water to the kettle during steaming so it does not dry out.

Half an hour before the end of cooking add green peas to melon with salt and monosodium glutamate and enough chicken stock to fill melon three-quarters full again.

To serve: remove melon in its dish or pan from kettle and sprinkle with chopped mandarin peel, serve, using the melon cup as a tureen. Ladle a few of the diced ingredients with the soup into each bowl and add a piece of the tender melon flesh.

Sai Yong Choy Yuke Gung
(Watercress Beef Soup)

2 bunches of watercress
2–3 cooked beef rib bones
5 cups boiling water
$\frac{1}{2}$ teaspoon monosodium glutamate
salt

Method
Wash watercress thoroughly and cut into 4 inch sprigs. Combine it in a kettle with the remaining ingredients and salt to taste. Cover and boil rapidly for 30 minutes; skim any fat from the soup. Remove bones and serve.

Chinese Chicken Stock

3–4 lb roasting chicken or fowl (including giblets)
2 stalks of celery
2 scallions, chopped
$\frac{1}{2}$ teaspoon salt
$\frac{1}{2}$ teaspoon monosodium glutamate

Method
Put chicken in a kettle with giblets (except heart and liver) and water to cover. Add a lid, bring to a boil, reduce heat and simmer 2–3 hours, adding more boiling water as liquid in kettle evaporates. Add remaining ingredients and simmer 30 minutes longer. Strain, chill and skim off fat before using.

Chinese Soup Stock

1 chicken carcass
$\frac{1}{2}$ lb lean pork or 2 lb pork bones
$\frac{1}{2}$ teaspoon salt
$\frac{1}{2}$ teaspoon monosodium glutamate

Method
Rub or toss salt and monosodium glutamate with pork or pork bones. Put them in a kettle with the chicken carcass and water to cover, add a lid and bring to a boil. Reduce heat and simmer 2 hours, adding more boiling water as liquid in kettle evaporates. Strain, chill and skim off fat before using.

Mo Gwa Bok Opp Tong
(Fuzzy Squash and Pigeon Soup)

2 medium fuzzy squash, peeled and halved
1 large pigeon
2 quarts Chinese chicken stock
1 inch square dried mandarin peel, softened in cold water and drained
salt (to taste)

Method
Put pigeon with chicken stock in a large kettle and bring to a boil. Reduce heat, skim off any fat and add prepared squash and mandarin peel. Cover pan and simmer 2 hours. Add salt to taste and serve, giving each person a piece of fuzzy squash and some meat from the pigeon.

The meat from the pigeon and squash is delicious when dipped in Chinese hot mustard and soy sauce, with chopsticks, between spoonsful of soup.
Note: when serving this soup Chinese-style in a large tureen, each person serves himself and pulls off some pigeon meat with his chopsticks.

Chinese hot mustard: mix hot, dry mustard to a paste with water to desired consistency and add a few drops of vegetable oil for smoothness. Use sparingly.

All Chinese recipes serve 4 people unless otherwise stated.

Yee Chee Tong
(Shark's Fin Soup)

4 large dried shark's fins
2 whole fresh ginger roots
1 onion, peeled
8 cups Chinese chicken
    stock with breast meat from
    chicken (shredded)
salt (to taste)
monosodium glutamate
    (to taste)

For garnish
½ cup finely shredded cooked
    Virginia ham
2–3 scallions, finely sliced

This recipe should be started 2 days before serving. Serves 4–6 people.

Method
Put shark's fins in a large roasting pan or baking dish, cover with boiling water and let soak for 8 hours. Wash, rinse and repeat soaking and rinsing process.

Put shark's fins in a large kettle with 1 ginger root, cover with water, add a lid and simmer 3 hours. Cool, then remove and discard all skin, bones, flesh and liquid, reserving the golden brown cartilages. Drain these thoroughly and put in a smaller pan with remaining ginger root and whole onion. Cover with water, add a lid and simmer 5 hours. Remove and rinse cartilages and simmer again with onion and ginger root in water to cover for 5 hours. Discard liquid, ginger and onion but reserve cartilages.

Put chicken stock in a kettle with cartilages and chicken breast meat. Cover, simmer 30 minutes, add salt and monosodium glutamate to taste.

To serve: transfer hot soup to a tureen and sprinkle with Virginia ham and scallion.

Shark's fin is a supreme delicacy. It is a classic part of Chinese banquet menus. Top quality fin, yielding 5 inch strands, is expensive – a restaurant serving can cost as much as $50; average quality fin, in 2–3 inch strands, is about one-quarter the price and even the least expensive grade – a 1 inch strand, is a luxury.

Don Fah Tong
(Egg Flower Soup)

2 eggs, beaten to mix
5 cups Chinese chicken stock
1 cup frozen peas, thawed
½ cup canned diced button
    mushrooms, drained
¼ cup diced uncooked chicken
salt (to taste)
monosodium glutamate
    (to taste)

Method
Put stock in a kettle, cover and bring to a boil. Add peas, mushrooms and chicken. Pour in beaten eggs and stir until they separate in shreds. Add salt and monosodium glutamate and serve at once.

Bok Fon
(Steamed Rice)

2 cups long grain rice
water

Tall, deep pan with heavy bottom and tight-fitting lid

Be sure to use Texas Patna or Louisiana long grain rice – not round grain or pearl grain – for steaming.

Method
Wash rice thoroughly in 4–5 changes of water, rubbing it between your hands until the water is no longer milky. Drain rice thoroughly and put in the pan with water to come about 1 inch above the rice.

Cover the pan tightly and bring water to a rolling boil. Continue cooking until all water has evaporated (about 15 minutes), turn heat as low as possible and cook rice 15 minutes longer. The excess water absorbed by the rice during vigorous boiling will evaporate, leaving rice tender and each grain separate. Fluff rice with chopsticks or a fork before serving.

To keep rice hot: leave pan covered after cooking and stand on an asbestos mat over low heat.

Yeong Jow Chow Fon
(Yeong Jow Fried Rice)

3 cups cold (steamed) rice
2–3 tablespoons vegetable oil
¼ cup diced uncooked, peeled
    shrimps
½ teaspoon salt
¼ cup diced barbecued pork,
    or cooked ham
2 scallions, trimmed and cut
    in fine slices
¼ cup cooked green peas
1 cup shredded lettuce
2 tablespoons soy sauce

The vegetables, meat and seafood combined in this dish make it ideal for a 1-dish meal. If serving rice as an accompaniment to another dish, omit shrimps and ham, if you like.

Method
In a wok or heavy skillet, heat 2 tablespoons oil until sizzling. Add shrimps and salt and toss and turn for 2–3 minutes or until cooked. Add pork or ham, scallions, green peas, lettuce and rice and sprinkle over soy sauce. Blend in well.

Press rice gently into pan and fry for a few seconds; turn and repeat the process until all rice is heated, then turn and mix it rapidly for 5–7 minutes, adding a few drops more oil if necessary to prevent burning. Serve at once.

All Chinese recipes serve 4 people unless otherwise stated.

Gwai Fah Don
(Precious Flower Egg)

6 eggs, beaten to mix
$\frac{1}{2}$ cup finely sliced bamboo
    shoots
$\frac{1}{4}$ cup finely sliced fresh
    snow peas
$\frac{1}{2}$ cup finely sliced onion
$\frac{1}{4}$ cup dried Chinese black
    mushrooms, soaked, drained
    and thinly sliced
4–6 small thin slices of
    barbecued pork, or cooked
    ham
2 tablespoons oil
$\frac{1}{2}$ teaspoon salt
$\frac{1}{4}$ teaspoon monosodium
    glutamate

Method
Heat a wok or heavy skillet,
add the oil and salt, mix well
and heat until sizzling. Add
the bamboo shoots, peas,
onion, mushrooms and pork
or ham and toss and turn over
high heat for 5 minutes or
until ingredients are almost
cooked. Add the beaten egg,
mixed with the monosodium
glutamate, reduce the heat to
medium high and turn and mix
gently like an omelet until the
eggs are just set. Slide onto a
warm platter and serve with
hot steamed or fried rice.

Gawn Jeen Hah Look
(Dry Fried Shrimps in Shell)

$1\frac{1}{2}$ lb uncooked, unpeeled
    jumbo shrimps, washed
    and well drained
2 tablespoons oil
$\frac{1}{3}$ teaspoon salt
1 teaspoon soy sauce
2 tablespoons chicken stock
3 large scallions, cut into
    2 inch pieces discarding
    green top (for scallion
    brushes)

Method
In a wok or large heavy skillet,
mix the oil and salt thoroughly
and heat until sizzling. With
long chopsticks or tongs, place
shrimps flat in the pan. Fry
2–3 minutes on each side until
shells are brown.

Add soy sauce, chicken
stock and scallion brushes;
toss and turn with chopsticks
or a ladle over high heat until
all ingredients are very hot
and well blended. Serve at
once, leaving guests to shell
their own shrimps.

With ladle and chopsticks, toss
shrimps in wok over high heat
to blend with other ingredients

Scallion Brushes
Cut off the root and trim
the stalk to make about 2
inches of scallion. With a
sharp knife cut thin slivers
almost but not quite
through both stalk and
root end so the slivers
are held together in the
middle. Toss in ice
water for curly brush or
fringe effect.

Yeong Loong Hah Mei
(Stuffed Lobster Tails)

4 large lobster tails
$\frac{1}{2}$ lb ground pork
$\frac{1}{4}$ cup black bean paste
$\frac{1}{4}$ cup dried Chinese
    mushrooms, soaked, drained
    and finely chopped
$\frac{1}{4}$ cup water chestnuts,
    drained and finely chopped
3 tablespoons oil
$\frac{1}{2}$ teaspoon salt
$\frac{1}{2}$ teaspoon monosodium
    glutamate
1 clove of garlic, crushed
$\frac{1}{2}$ cup water
2 tablespoons soy sauce
1 teaspoon cornstarch

Method
Cut along the underside membrane of the lobster tails and
remove the meat, leaving the
shells intact. Reserve shells
and finely chop the meat.

Heat a wok or large heavy
skillet, add 1 tablespoon oil
and heat until sizzling. Add
the ground pork and cook,
turning, stirring to break up
the pieces, until browned.
Cover and cook 5 minutes;
take from heat and let cool.

In a bowl mix lobster meat,
cooled cooked pork, mush-
rooms and water chestnuts.

Add the salt and mono-
sodium glutamate and mix
with the hands until thoroughly blended. Separate into
4 portions, roll each portion
into a ball and throw them
firmly onto a chopping board
10–15 times until the mixture
is pliable. Shape each portion
to fill the lobster tails evenly
and arrange on a heatproof
dish.

Heat a wok or skillet, add
remaining oil and stir in the
bean paste and garlic. Cook,
tossing and turning, until the
garlic is browned. Mix the
soy sauce and water with the
cornstarch to a smooth paste
and add to the wok. Cook,
stirring, until the sauce
thickens and spread it over
each stuffed lobster tail.
Steam the tails over boiling
water in a covered pan for
20 minutes and serve hot
with steamed rice.

Try dry fried shrimps in shell (page 67) or beef casserole with rice

Ngow Yuke Fon
(Beef Casserole with Rice)

1 lb top round of beef, cut in
    thin strips 1 inch wide
3 cups hot steamed rice
2 tablespoons vegetable oil
3 scallions, trimmed and cut
    in 1–2 inch pieces
½ teaspoon salt
2 tablespoons oyster sauce
pinch of sugar
1 cup hot chicken stock
1 tablespoon cornstarch (mixed
    to a paste with 1 tablespoon
    water)
1 egg, to serve (optional)

Method
In a wok or skillet heat oil. When sizzling hot, add sliced beef and brown rapidly, turning and mixing for 1 minute only. Take out and reserve. Add scallions, salt, oyster sauce, sugar and chicken stock to pan and turn and mix over high heat for 1 minute. Put back the beef, gradually stir in cornstarch paste and turn and mix the ingredients rapidly for 2–3 minutes until the sauce thickens.

Fluff rice with chopsticks or a fork and place in a casserole. Pour the hot beef with the sauce over it, crack the egg and drop it in the center, if you like, and serve.

Jing Lo Yee
(Striped Bass à la Kan)

4 striped bass steaks, cut
    ¾–1 inch thick
1 clove of garlic, crushed
2 tablespoons black bean paste
1 teaspoon sugar
4½ tablespoons soy sauce
3 tablespoons oil

For garnish
3–4 scallions, trimmed and
    finely sliced
few sprigs of Chinese
    parsley, washed

Method
Place fish steaks in a shallow baking dish. In a bowl thoroughly mix the garlic, black bean paste, sugar, soy sauce and oil and spread evenly over fish steaks. Set the dish on a rack in a large kettle, add ¾–1 inch hot water to kettle, cover with a tight-fitting lid and steam over high heat for 20 minutes – do not overcook.

Lift out the dish, garnish fish with scallion and parsley sprigs and serve with steamed rice.

Chow Yee Peen
(Fillets of Fish with Vegetables)

1 lb fish fillets (preferably
    striped bass or red snapper),
    cut in ¼ inch diagonal slices
½ cup sliced onion
½ cup sliced celery
½ cup sliced bamboo shoots
½ cup canned water chestnuts,
    drained and sliced
1 cup (¼ lb) button mushrooms,
    sliced
3 tablespoons oil
⅓ cup chicken stock
½ teaspoon salt
1 teaspoon soy sauce
1 teaspoon monosodium
    glutamate
1 teaspoon cornstarch (mixed
    to a paste with 1 tablespoon
    water)

Method
In a wok or large heavy skillet, heat 2 tablespoons of oil until sizzling. Add fish fillets, reduce heat to medium high and brown them rapidly first on one side, then on the other (no longer than 1 minute each side). Take from pan and reserve.

Add remaining oil to pan, heat until sizzling and add onion, celery, bamboo shoots, water chestnuts and mushrooms. Toss and turn 1 minute until all vegetables are blended, then add chicken stock, salt, soy sauce and monosodium glutamate. Cover and cook over high heat for about 5 minutes. Uncover. Replace fish, add cornstarch paste and toss and turn ingredients gently until thoroughly heated and sauce has thickened. Serve at once with steamed rice.

Jow Yeong Dow Foo
(Fish Stuffed in Bean Cake)

¾ lb fish fillets
    (use any kind of large
    fish that can be completely
    boned)
¾ lb uncooked, peeled shrimps
8 square bean cakes
½ teaspoon salt
⅓ teaspoon monosodium
    glutamate
1 egg white
deep fat (for frying)

Method
Chop fish and shrimps together very finely. Put in a bowl and stir in salt and monosodium glutamate. Beat egg white lightly until frothy and stir into fish mixture to bind it. Mix thoroughly with the hands and divide into 16 portions. Roll each portion into a ball; literally throw the balls firmly onto a chopping board 15–20 times until the mixture is pliable and all air is knocked out.

Cut each square bean cake diagonally to form 2 triangles. Starting at the apex of each triangle, cut a slit three-quarters of the way inside to form a pocket, and stuff each triangle with a fish ball, flattening it slightly and smoothing it to the shape of the bean cake.

Heat deep fat to 350°F on a fat thermometer and fry the stuffed bean cake triangles a few at a time for 2–3 minutes or until barely golden. Drain on paper towels and serve.

All Chinese recipes serve 4 people unless otherwise stated.

Eat hot spicy curried crab in the shell with your fingers

Gah Lay Hai
(Curried Crab in Shell)

2 large live Dungeness crabs
$\frac{1}{4}$ cup oil
2 tablespoons curry powder
1 teaspoon salt
1 medium onion, sliced
2 medium green peppers,
   cored, seeded and cut in
   $\frac{1}{2}$ inch squares
2 large tomatoes, peeled,
   seeded and cut in 8 wedges
1 teaspoon sugar
1 teaspoon monosodium
   glutamate
2 cups chicken stock
2 tablespoons cornstarch
   (mixed to a paste with 2
   tablespoons water)

When live Dungeness crabs are not available, 2 live $1-1\frac{1}{2}$ lb lobsters may be substituted. Serves 4–6 people.

Method
Wearing heavy gloves, hold each crab firmly in a cloth and scrub it under cold water. If the crab is moving strongly, kill it by piercing the under-shell behind the eyes. Remove the flat under-shell and reserve the brown creamy part or crab fat (custard). Remove and crack the legs and claws and cut at the joints. Discard the lungs or 'dead men's fingers', clean the body of each crab and cut it (including shell) into thirds.

In a wok or heavy skillet, heat oil, curry powder and salt thoroughly, stirring for $\frac{1}{2}$ minute or until sizzling. Add the body and cracked crab pieces, onion, green pepper, tomatoes, sugar and mono-sodium glutamate.

Stir a little stock into the crab fat until soft and add to pan with remaining stock. Turn all ingredients until well mixed, cover and cook over high heat for 12–15 minutes or until crab meat is cooked.

Remove lid and gradually add cornstarch paste, turning constantly until curry sauce thickens; the crab should be thoroughly coated with sauce.

Serve crab very hot with steamed rice. Eat the crab with your fingers and pass hot damp towels when the crab is finished.

Hop To Gai Kow
(Walnut Chicken)

1 cup boneless uncooked
   chicken, cut into $\frac{3}{4}$ inch
   squares, $\frac{1}{4}$ inch thick
1 cup walnut halves
$\frac{1}{4}$ cup canned bamboo shoots,
   drained and cut in $\frac{3}{4}$ inch
   squares, $\frac{1}{8}$ inch thick
$\frac{1}{4}$ cup oil
$\frac{1}{4}$ teaspoon salt
1 teaspoon soy sauce
$\frac{1}{4}$ teaspoon monosodium
   glutamate
$\frac{3}{4}$ cup chicken stock
2 tablespoons cornstarch
   (mixed to a paste with
   2 tablespoons water)

Method
Fry walnuts in 2 tablespoons oil until crisp and drain them on paper towels. Heat a wok or heavy skillet, add the remaining 2 tablespoons oil with the salt, stir until well mixed and heat until sizzling. Add the chicken and toss and turn over high heat for 1 minute. Add the soy sauce, mono-sodium glutamate and bamboo slices and toss over high heat for 1 minute more. Add the chicken stock, cover and cook over high heat for 2–3 minutes. Add the walnut halves and mix well.

Gradually add the corn-starch paste and toss and turn for about 2 minutes or until the sauce thickens. Serve with steamed or fried rice.

Sesame Seeds

To toast: heat a small skillet and toast the sesame seeds without oil, stirring constantly until they are evenly browned.

Gee Mah Gai
(Sesame Chicken)

$3\frac{1}{2}$–4 lb roasting chicken
1 egg, beaten to mix
4 drops of gin
salt and pepper
2 tablespoons water chestnut
   flour or cornstarch
oil (for frying)

For sauce
1 tablespoon sesame seeds,
   toasted (see box)
2 cups water
$\frac{1}{2}$ cup half and half
1 cup ($\frac{1}{4}$ lb) diced mushrooms
2 tablespoons cornstarch
$\frac{1}{2}$ teaspoon monosodium
   glutamate
1 teaspoon salt

Method
Cut meat from the chicken in as large pieces as possible, discarding skin and bone. Cut chicken meat in $\frac{1}{4}$ inch slices. Mix egg and gin with a little salt and pepper, toss the chicken in it and let stand 10 minutes. Add chestnut flour or cornstarch and toss until coated. In a large skillet heat 1 inch oil until it sizzles when a piece of chicken is added. Gently lower in the chicken pieces, stir to separate them and fry 5 minutes or until lightly browned. Lift out the chicken and drain it on paper towels. Transfer to a platter and keep warm.

To make sauce: in a sauce-pan stir water into cornstarch until smooth. Add the half and half, mushrooms, mono-sodium glutamate and salt and heat, stirring, until the sauce thickens. Spoon sauce over the chicken, sprinkle with sesame seeds and serve.

All Chinese recipes serve 4 people unless otherwise stated.

Goon Yin-Yin Yang Gai
(Chicken à la Kan)

3–3½ lb chicken
5–6 thin slices of Virginia
    ham, cut into 1½ X 2 inch
    rectangles
1 tablespoon oil
salt
1 lb Chinese broccoli, washed,
    stems peeled and cut in
    2 inch lengths
1 teaspoon soy sauce
pinch of sugar
pinch of monosodium
    glutamate
¼ cup chicken stock
1 tablespoon cornstarch
    (mixed to a paste with 1
    tablespoon water)
broccoli flowers (for
    decoration)

For chicken sauce
½ cup chicken stock
¼ teaspoon soy sauce
¼ teaspoon monosodium
    glutamate
½ teaspoon cornstarch
    (mixed to a paste with 1
    teaspoon water)

This formal dish is popular at wedding banquets. The ham symbolizes Yin (male) and the chicken Yang (female).

Method
Put chicken in a kettle with salted water to cover, add lid and simmer 40–50 minutes or until just tender. Drain chicken and run under cold water until cool.

With a sharp cleaver remove chicken legs and cut out the bones, leaving meat as intact as possible. Reshape legs and slice each in 4 neat pieces. Remove breast meat from the bone and slice each breast into 3–4 pieces. With a cleaver, carefully scoop up the sections of chicken so they keep their natural shape and slide them onto a hot platter. Insert a piece of ham between each piece of chicken; keep in a warm place.

In a wok or heavy skillet, heat oil and ½ teaspoon salt until sizzling. Add broccoli, 1 teaspoon soy sauce, sugar and pinch of monosodium glutamate and toss and mix over high heat for 1 minute. Add the ¼ cup chicken stock, cover and cook for 2 minutes. Uncover and stir in cornstarch paste (made using 1 tablespoon cornstarch). Continue to toss over high heat until sauce thickens and is well blended with broccoli. Spoon broccoli around chicken and ham and keep hot.

To make chicken sauce: in a small saucepan put chicken stock, ¼ teaspoon salt, soy sauce and monosodium glutamate and bring to a boil. Gradually stir in cornstarch paste (from ½ teaspoon cornstarch) and cook until sauce thickens. Spoon sauce over chicken and ham (not over broccoli), decorate dish with broccoli flowers and serve at once.

Broccoli Flowers

Cut broccoli stalks into 2½ inch lengths and peel them. Lay stalks on a chopping board and slash down lengthwise into ¼ inch slices leaving them joined at one end. Give the stalk a half turn to lie flat and make a similar series of cuts so stalk is divided into narrower sticks still joined at one end. Soak the stalk in ice water for 1 hour, or until cut ends curl to a flower shape.

Cutting up Cooked Chicken or Duck

Remove wings and legs. With a sharp cleaver split bird lengthwise down the spine and breastbone. Cut each half in two crosswise then, with quick strokes, chop the quarters through the bone into 1 inch wide pieces. With the cleaver scoop quarters onto a platter, reshaping the bird. Cut legs and wings in half and arrange them in their natural position on each side of the bird.

All Chinese recipes serve 4 people unless otherwise stated.

Nom Moong Gai
(Hong Kong Lemon Chicken)

3½–4 lb roasting chicken
12 star anise (bot gok),
    washed and crushed
½ teaspoon ground cinnamon
1 teaspoon finely chopped
    fresh ginger root
1 teaspoon dried mandarin
    peel, soaked and finely
    chopped
2 cloves of garlic, crushed
½ bunch of Chinese parsley,
    washed and chopped
1 teaspoon salt
½ teaspoon monosodium
    glutamate
1 teaspoon sugar
1 lemon, thinly sliced
1–2 tablespoons uncolored
    natural soy sauce (for
    rubbing)
1 tablespoon cornstarch
deep fat (for frying)
grated rind and juice of ½ lemon
2 teaspoons cornstarch
    (mixed to a paste with 2
    teaspoons water)
1 lemon, cut in wedges (for
    garnish)

Method
In a bowl mix anise, cinammon, ginger root, mandarin peel, garlic, parsley, salt, monosodium glutamate, sugar and sliced lemon. Place chicken in a deep thin baking dish or pan and spread anise mixture evenly all over its surface. Lower dish into a large kettle with a rack in the bottom, add ¾–1 inch hot water to the kettle, cover tightly and steam chicken for 10 minutes. Turn chicken over, and steam again for 10 minutes longer. Take out chicken and discard flavorings. Strain the juices in the dish and reserve for the sauce.

Rub chicken with soy sauce and sprinkle evenly with cornstarch. Put chicken in a clean deep baking dish or pan and continue steaming for 10 minutes longer. Cool it.

Heat a pan of deep fat, large enough to cover the whole chicken, to 350°F on a fat thermometer. Carefully lower in chicken and fry for 3–4 minutes or until golden brown. Take out and drain on paper towels. Cut chicken into pieces for serving and arrange on a platter.

In a saucepan heat reserved chicken juices with lemon rind and juice. When boiling, stir in cornstarch paste and cook until sauce thickens slightly. Strain the sauce and spoon it over the chicken, garnish with lemon wedges and serve.

So See Gai
(Coriander Chicken Salad)

3½–4 lb roasting chicken, cut in half and back bone discarded
bunch of Chinese parsley (coriander), washed and stems removed
8–10 scallions, finely shredded lengthwise
1 tablespoon sesame seeds
1 tablespoon Chinese hot mustard (see page 65)
½ head Boston lettuce, shredded
½ teaspoon monosodium glutamate
½ teaspoon salt
½ teaspoon sugar
deep fat (for frying)

Method
Heat a large pan of deep fat to 350°F on a fat thermometer, gently put in the chicken and fry 8–10 minutes or until golden brown and tender. Drain well on paper towels and cool.

Take chicken meat from the bones, discard the skin, and pull meat into shreds with the fingers. Mix the chicken with the mustard, then with the sesame seeds. Add sugar, monosodium glutamate and salt to taste, Chinese parsley (reserve a few sprigs for garnish) and green onions and toss in a salad bowl until thoroughly mixed. Line a platter with shredded lettuce and pile the chicken mixture on top. Garnish the chicken with Chinese parsley and serve.

Bok Opp Soong
(Squab in Lettuce Cups)

3 squabs
1 head Boston lettuce
1 lb fresh water chestnuts, washed, peeled and diced, or 2 cups canned water chestnuts, drained and diced
6 dried Chinese black mushrooms, soaked in water, drained and diced
½ cup diced celery
2 tablespoons diced lean pork
2 teaspoons diced smoked Chinese duck liver (optional)
½ cup diced bamboo shoots
¼ cup oil
pinch of salt
1 cup chicken stock
1 teaspoon soy sauce
pinch of pepper
½ teaspoon monosodium glutamate
1 tablespoon cornstarch (mixed to a paste with 1 tablespoon water)

Method
Wash the lettuce, dividing it into leaves and crisp the leaves in the refrigerator. Remove the squab meat from the bones, discarding the skin, and chop it finely.

Heat a skillet, add the oil and heat slightly. Add the squab and pork and toss and turn over high heat for 2 minutes. Add the water chestnuts, mushrooms, celery, duck liver, if using, and bamboo shoots, reduce the heat to medium and toss and mix for 2 minutes. Add the chicken stock, soy sauce, pepper and monosodium glutamate, stir until mixed, cover and cook over medium heat for 10 minutes. Gradually add the cornstarch paste and toss and turn until the mixture is very hot. Transfer to a serving dish and serve with the lettuce leaves in a separate bowl. Each guest takes a lettuce leaf, places 2 tablespoons of the soong in it and eats it with his hands.

Serve the Chinese roast duck, carved and reshaped, with fried rice and plum sauce

Faw Opp
(Chinese Roast Duck)

Specialty Chinese markets sell ducks already roasted, with their juices in a separate container.

To serve: cut up the duck and transfer pieces to a platter. Heat duck juices, pour over the duck and garnish dish with scallion brushes. Give each person a dish of plum sauce (see mouie jeong) for dipping and serve steamed or fried rice separately.

Star anise have a licorice flavor and smell. They come from a small evergreen tree that grows in southwestern China and when ripe, the fruits blossom into the form of a star.

Leen Gee Opp
(Lotus Stuffed Duck)

4–5 lb duck, boned
2–3 teaspoons soy sauce (for rubbing)
2 cups oil
½ bunch of Chinese parsley, washed and chopped
2 scallions, trimmed and sliced
10 star anise broken into small pieces
1 inch piece mandarin peel, soaked and chopped
bunch of Chinese parsley (for garnish)

For stuffing
1 cup canned leen gee (lotus nuts), washed
1 cup pearl barley, soaked overnight and drained
1 cup fresh or canned ginkgo nuts
1 cup dried Chinese mushrooms, soaked until softened and cut in ¼ inch cubes
½ teaspoon monosodium glutamate
¼ cup diced cooked ham
1½ teaspoons salt
½ teaspoon sugar

For sauce
2 cups Chinese chicken stock
¼ teaspoon salt
¼ teaspoon soy sauce
pinch of pepper
2 teaspoons cornstarch (mixed to a paste with 2 teaspoons water)

Trussing needle and string

Method
Dry boned duck thoroughly with paper towels.

To make stuffing: shell fresh ginkgo nuts or drain canned ones. Mix softened barley with lotus nuts, mushrooms, ginkgo nuts, monosodium glutamate, ham, salt and sugar until well blended. Spread stuffing on boned duck and sew up with a trussing needle and string, reshaping bird to its original shape. Rub skin with soy sauce.

In a large pan heat the oil, add duck and brown carefully all over; drain on paper towels. Place duck in a deep baking dish or thin pan and scatter over the Chinese parsley, scallions, anise and mandarin peel. Set the dish on a trivet or a rack in a large kettle and add 2–3 inches hot water to the kettle — the dish should not be in contact with the water. Cover kettle tightly and steam duck for 3 hours, adding more hot water to prevent it from drying out. Remove duck and discard topping. Discard trussing strings. Keep duck warm.

To make sauce: bring chicken stock to a boil in a saucepan and add the salt, soy sauce and pepper. Gradually stir in cornstarch paste and cook until sauce thickens. Keep hot.

Set duck on a hot platter, pour over sauce and garnish with Chinese parsley. To serve, cut duck crosswise into slices.

Ho Yow Ngow Yuke
(Oyster Sauce Beef)

1 lb fillet or strip steak, sliced ¼ inch thick and cut in 2 X 1 inch pieces
¼ teaspoon salt
½ teaspoon soy sauce
1 teaspoon cornstarch
pinch of sugar
2 tablespoons oil
6–8 scallions, cut into 1 inch pieces, discarding green tops
2 tablespoons oyster sauce
¼ cup chicken stock
½ teaspoon monosodium glutamate
1 tablespoon cornstarch (mixed to a paste with 1 tablespoon water)

Method
In a bowl mix salt, soy sauce, 1 teaspoon cornstarch and pinch of sugar. Add sliced beef, mix well and leave 5 minutes.

In a wok or large heavy skillet, heat oil until sizzling. Put in beef mixture with the scallions and oyster sauce and toss and turn over high heat for 3 minutes. Add chicken stock, monosodium glutamate and cornstarch paste and toss and mix until sauce thickens and the beef and scallions are well coated. Serve very hot with steamed rice (see page 66).

Fresh lychee nuts and chunks of pineapple are combined with cubes of pork to make lychee pineapple pork, sweet and sour

Lychee Baw Law Goo Lo Yuke
(Lychee Pineapple Pork Sweet and Sour)

15 fresh lychees, shelled and pitted, or 1 can (11 oz) lychees, drained
1 small pineapple, peeled, cored and cut in chunks or 1 can (14 oz) pineapple chunks, drained and syrup reserved
1 lb lean pork, cut in $\frac{3}{4}$ inch cubes
1 egg, beaten to mix
1 cup flour
$\frac{1}{2}$ teaspoon monosodium glutamate
salt and pepper
deep fat (for frying)
1 teaspoon soy sauce
$\frac{1}{2}$ cup sugar
$\frac{1}{4}$ cup ketchup
$\frac{1}{2}$ cup white vinegar
2 tablespoons cornstarch (mixed to a paste with 2 tablespoons water)
1 medium green pepper, cored, seeded and cut in $\frac{1}{2}$ inch squares

Method
Dip pork cubes in the beaten egg so they are well coated.

In a bowl mix flour, monosodium glutamate and $\frac{1}{2}$ teaspoon salt together. Add pork and mix until well coated.

Heat a pan of deep fat to 360°F on a fat thermometer, add the pork and fry 6–8 minutes until browned. Take out, drain on paper towels and keep warm.

In a wok or deep skillet mix soy sauce, sugar, ketchup and vinegar with $\frac{1}{3}$ cup of the reserved pineapple syrup and bring to a boil; taste for seasoning. Gradually stir in cornstarch paste and cook until mixture thickens. Add pork, lychees, pineapple chunks and green pepper and turn and mix over high heat for

5 minutes or until all ingredients are very hot. Serve with steamed rice.

Lop Cheong Jing Gee Yuke Beong
(Steamed Pork Patty with Chinese Sausage)

1$\frac{1}{2}$ lb pork, including some fat, finely chopped
4 Chinese dried sausages, cut diagonally in $\frac{1}{2}$ inch slices
$\frac{1}{2}$ teaspoon salt
1 teaspoon soy sauce
pinch of pepper
pinch of monosodium glutamate
1$\frac{1}{2}$ teaspoons cornstarch

Method
In a bowl mix pork, salt, soy sauce, pepper, monosodium glutamate and cornstarch. When very well blended, transfer to a heatproof platter and press into one large patty about $\frac{1}{2}$ inch thick. Press sausages on top of the patty.

Place patty on a wire rack in a large kettle, add $\frac{3}{4}$–1 inch hot water, cover kettle and steam over high heat for 25 minutes or until pork and sausages are thoroughly cooked, adding more hot water to pan when necessary. Serve at once with steamed rice.

All Chinese recipes serve 4 people unless otherwise stated.

See Jup Pai Gwut
(Spareribs with Black Bean Sauce)

2 lb spareribs, cut into 1$\frac{1}{2}$ inch lengths
2 teaspoons black bean paste
$\frac{1}{4}$ teaspoon finely chopped fresh ginger root
3 cloves of garlic, crushed
1 teaspoon soy sauce
2 tablespoons oil
$\frac{1}{2}$ teaspoon monosodium glutamate
$\frac{1}{2}$ teaspoon salt
1$\frac{1}{2}$–2 cups Chinese chicken stock
black pepper, freshly ground (to taste)
2 tablespoons cornstarch (mixed to a paste with 2 tablespoons water)
1 large green pepper, cored, seeded and cut in 1 inch squares
3 scallion tops, cut in 1 inch pieces

This recipe has quite a different flavor if 2 tablespoons red bean cake (nom yee) are used instead of the 2 teaspoons black bean paste. It reheats well and the flavor mellows when the dish is kept overnight.

Method
Boil spareribs in water for 15 minutes, drain and rinse in cold water. Mix bean paste with the ginger root, garlic and soy sauce.

In a wok or large heavy skillet, heat oil until sizzling. Add pieces of spareribs and brown them quickly on both sides, turning with chopsticks or tongs. Add bean paste mixture with monosodium glutamate and salt, toss and mix for 1 minute over high heat and add 1$\frac{1}{2}$ cups chicken stock and freshly ground black pepper to taste. Cover and cook over high heat for

25 minutes or until spareribs are thoroughly cooked, turning occasionally and adding more chicken stock if the liquid evaporates too fast.

Gradually add cornstarch paste and turn and mix over high heat until sauce thickens. Add green pepper and scallions, heat thoroughly and serve with steamed rice.

Dow Foo Yuke
(Bean Cake Sautéed with Meat)

8 square bean cakes (dow foo)
8–10 small thin slices of uncooked pork or ham
2 tablespoons oil
2 scallions, trimmed and cut in $\frac{3}{4}$ inch pieces
1 teaspoon bean sauce
$\frac{1}{2}$ teaspoon monosodium glutamate
$\frac{1}{2}$ teaspoon salt
$\frac{1}{2}$ cup Chinese chicken stock
2 teaspoons cornstarch (mixed to a paste with 2 teaspoons water)

Method
Slice each bean cake into 6 pieces.

In a wok or heavy skillet, heat oil until sizzling. Add pork or ham and cook over high heat for 2–3 minutes or until brown on both sides.

Add bean cakes, scallions and bean sauce. Reduce heat to medium high and turn and mix gently for 10 minutes without breaking up the bean cakes. Add monosodium glutamate, salt and chicken stock and continue to turn and mix gently over high heat for 5 minutes or until very hot. Gradually add cornstarch paste; cook until sauce is thick and all ingredients coated. Serve at once with steamed or yeong jow fried rice (see page 66).

Ho Bow Don
(Oyster Purse Eggs)

8 eggs
8 teaspoons oyster sauce
1 teaspoon oil

Method
In a wok or skillet, heat oil slightly. Fry the eggs, sunny side up, over medium heat. When they are almost done, pour 1 teaspoon oyster sauce over each egg yolk and fold whites over on top.

Set each egg on top of a small bowl of steamed rice and serve each person 2 bowls.

Sah Bok Jing Don
(Steamed Eggs with Clams)

4 large eggs, beaten to mix
1 can (8 oz) minced clams, drained and juice reserved
$\frac{1}{2}$ teaspoon monosodium glutamate
$\frac{1}{4}$ teaspoon salt

For garnish
1 tablespoon soy or oyster sauce
2–3 scallions, trimmed and finely sliced
bunch of Chinese parsley, washed

Shallow ovenproof dish (1$\frac{1}{2}$ quart capacity)

Method
In a saucepan mix the clam juice with enough water to make 2$\frac{1}{2}$ cups. Bring to a boil, then let cool. Lightly oil the dish.

In a bowl mix eggs, minced clams, monosodium glutamate and salt and stir in clam juice and water. Mix thoroughly and pour into the prepared dish. Place on a wire rack in a large kettle, add $\frac{3}{4}$–1 inch hot water to kettle, cover tightly and steam for 15–20 minutes over medium heat or until a knife inserted in the center comes out clean. Remove cover of pan often to drain off moisture that collects inside it.

Just before serving, trail soy or oyster sauce over the dish and garnish with sliced scallions and sprigs of Chinese parsley. Serve hot with steamed rice.

Yow Yim Bok Choy
(Chinese Chard with Oil and Salt)

1$\frac{1}{2}$ lb Chinese chard, washed and cut in 2 X $\frac{1}{2}$ inch pieces
2 tablespoons oil
2 cloves of garlic, crushed
$\frac{1}{2}$ teaspoon salt
$\frac{1}{2}$ teaspoon soy sauce
$\frac{1}{4}$ teaspoon monosodium glutamate
$\frac{1}{4}$ cup Chinese chicken stock
1 tablespoon cornstarch (mixed to a paste with 1 tablespoon water) – optional

This simple dish is one of the tests of a good Chinese cook – the chard should be glistening, hot and crunchy and it takes experience to time it just right. The amount of chicken stock may be reduced and little or no cornstarch added, if you prefer.

Method
In a wok or heavy skillet, heat oil, add garlic and salt and cook, stirring, over high heat until the garlic is browned. Add the chard, soy sauce and monosodium glutamate, toss and turn for 1 minute and add the chicken stock.

Cover pan and cook over high heat for 3 minutes, turn down the heat to medium and gradually add cornstarch paste, if you like. Toss and mix rapidly for 1–2 minutes until sauce thickens. Serve as a vegetable entrée with steamed rice.

Foo Gwa Gai Kow
(Bitter Melon with Chicken)

1$\frac{1}{2}$ lb Chinese bitter melon
2 small boneless chicken breasts or thighs, cut in $\frac{1}{2}$ inch cubes
2 tablespoons oil
$\frac{1}{2}$ teaspoon salt
4 cloves of garlic, crushed
2 tablespoons black bean paste
$\frac{1}{4}$ teaspoon soy sauce
pinch of monosodium glutamate
pinch of pepper
$\frac{1}{2}$ teaspoon sugar
$\frac{1}{2}$ cup Chinese chicken stock
1 tablespoon cornstarch (mixed to a paste with 1 tablespoon water)

Method
Cut melon in half, discard the seeds and slice flesh into $\frac{1}{4}$ inch thick pieces. Blanch in boiling water for 2 minutes and drain.

In a wok or heavy skillet, heat oil, add salt, garlic and black bean paste and cook, stirring, over high heat, until garlic is browned. Add blanched melon pieces, chicken, soy sauce, monosodium glutamate, pepper and sugar and toss and turn over high heat for 1 minute. Add chicken stock, cover and cook for 3 minutes.

Gradually add cornstarch paste and toss and mix for 2 minutes or until sauce is thickened and the melon and chicken are well coated. Serve with steamed rice.

All Chinese recipes serve 4 people unless otherwise stated.

Before serving steamed eggs with clams, pour a trail of soy or oyster sauce down the center of the dish

Leo Soon Gai Kow
(Fresh Asparagus Chicken with Black Bean Sauce)

1½ lb fresh asparagus
2 small boneless chicken breasts, cut in ¾ inch squares
1½ tablespoons black bean paste
1 clove of garlic, crushed
1 tablespoon soy sauce
pinch of monosodium glutamate
2 tablespoons oil
½ teaspoon salt
½ cup Chinese chicken stock
½ teaspoon sugar
1 tablespoon cornstarch (mixed to a paste with 1 tablespoon water) – optional

Method
Cut asparagus spears at the base to remove the tough ends and slice tender part of the spears diagonally into ½ inch slices. Blanch in boiling water for exactly 2 minutes, then drain.

Mix bean paste with garlic, soy sauce and monosodium glutamate.

In a wok or heavy skillet, mix oil and salt well and heat until sizzling. Add asparagus, chicken, bean paste mixture, chicken stock and sugar and toss and turn over high heat quickly but carefully for 1 minute. Cover and cook 2 minutes. Uncover, gradually add the cornstarch paste, if you like, and continue to cook, tossing and turning, until sauce is slightly thickened and coats the chicken and asparagus. Serve at once with steamed rice.

For the asparagus chicken make black bean paste mixture

Toss the asparagus, chicken and black bean paste mixture over high heat

Lon Dow Jook Soon Ma Tai
(Snow Peas with Water Chestnuts and Bamboo Shoots)

½ lb fresh snow peas, washed, tips and strings removed
½ cup fresh water chestnuts, washed, peeled and sliced, or ½ cup canned water chestnuts, drained and sliced
1 cup bamboo shoots, sliced ¼ inch thick and cut in 1 inch squares
2 tablespoons oil
4 thin slices of garlic (optional)
½ teaspoon salt
1 teaspoon soy sauce
2 tablespoons Chinese chicken stock
1 teaspoon cornstarch (mixed to a paste with 1 teaspoon water)

Method
In a wok or heavy skillet, heat oil, add garlic and salt and cook over high heat until garlic is browned. Add snow peas, water chestnuts, bamboo shoots and soy sauce and toss and turn over high heat for 1 minute. Add chicken stock, cover and cook 2 minutes.

Gradually add cornstarch paste; cook, turning, not longer than 1 minute until sauce thickens and all vegetables are coated. Serve as a vegetable entrée.

Baw Choy Foo Yee
(Spinach with Bean Cake Sauce)

2 lb fresh spinach, thoroughly washed and leaves halved
2 fermented bean cakes, mashed with 2 teaspoons juice from jar
3 tablespoons oil
1 teaspoon salt
2 cloves of garlic, crushed

Method
In a wok or heavy skillet, heat oil, add salt and garlic and cook over high heat until garlic is browned. Add spinach and bean cake paste and turn and mix until well blended.

Cover pan and cook over medium heat for 3 minutes. Turn the heat to high and toss and mix for 3 minutes longer. Serve with steamed rice.

Hung Gah Teem Choy
(Almond Blossom Dessert)

½ teaspoon almond extract
1 cup cold water
1 envelope gelatin
½ cup sugar
1 cup milk

4 individual custard cups

Method
In a saucepan sprinkle gelatin over ¼ cup of the cold water and let stand 5 minutes until spongy. Add remaining cold water and heat gently until gelatin dissolves. Add sugar and milk and stir over low heat until sugar is dissolved. Take from heat, stir in almond extract and pour into cups. Let stand until cool, then chill until set.

Coat asparagus chicken with black bean sauce; serve at once with steamed rice

Cole slaw and fruit salad (recipe is on page 84)

SIDE SALADS

Salads are ideal accompaniments for rich dishes. They provide a welcome astringency of flavor and their brilliant colors enliven any menu. In all salads, texture is important — cooked vegetables should be firm, not mushy, and crisp vegetables should be really crisp. Wash and chill fresh vegetables in the refrigerator or if necessary soak them in ice water for a short time. Make sure all ingredients are dry before adding dressing.

Remember to taste a salad for seasoning when it is complete — often a dressing that is perfectly seasoned on its own will taste bland when mixed with vegetables. Many of the following salads are also suitable as appetizers.

Vichy Salad

1 lb baby carrots
$\frac{3}{4}$ cup mayonnaise (mixed with 2 teaspoons Dijon-style mustard and 1 tablespoon heavy cream)
salt and pepper
1 tablespoon coarsely chopped parsley

Serve with cold roast pork, cold roast beef or cold chicken.

Method
Peel carrots and cut in julienne strips. Mix mayonnaise with mustard and cream and stir into carrots. Pile in a serving dish, season and sprinkle with parsley.

Lima Bean Salad

3 cups fresh shelled lima beans or 2 packages frozen lima beans
3–4 stalks of celery, sliced
1 small dill pickle, sliced
6 tablespoons vinaigrette dressing
1 tablespoon chopped chives

Serve with cold ham, tongue or corned beef.

Method
Cook the beans in boiling salted water for 15–20 minutes or until just tender or cook frozen lima beans according to package directions; drain, refresh and drain again. Mix the beans with the celery and dill pickle, pile in a salad bowl, spoon over the vinaigrette dressing, and sprinkle with chives.

Rice and Lima Bean Salad

1 cup rice
2 cups chicken stock
1$\frac{1}{2}$ cups shelled fresh baby lima beans or 1 package frozen baby lima beans
1–1$\frac{1}{4}$ cups mayonnaise
salt and pepper
juice of $\frac{1}{2}$ lemon (or to taste)

Serve with cold corned beef or with hot or cold roast lamb.

Method
Combine rice and stock in a pan, cover and simmer 15–18 minutes or until all the stock is absorbed and the rice is tender. Transfer to a bowl to cool.

Cook fresh limas in boiling salted water for 15–18 minutes or until just tender or cook frozen beans according to package directions; drain, refresh and drain again.

Mix the rice and beans with a fork and add enough mayonnaise to give a light, creamy consistency to the salad. Season well and add lemon juice to taste.

Vinaigrette Dressing

For $\frac{1}{2}$ cup: mix 2 tablespoons vinegar (any of the following types: red or white wine, cider or tarragon) with $\frac{1}{2}$ teaspoon salt and $\frac{1}{2}$ teaspoon freshly ground black pepper. Gradually add 6 tablespoons oil, preferably olive or peanut, whisking until dressing thickens slightly. Taste for seasoning.

Cole Slaw and Fruit Salad

$\frac{1}{2}$ firm head of green cabbage, shredded
$\frac{1}{2}$ lb seedless green grapes
$\frac{1}{2}$ lb black grapes
2 oranges
2 tangerines
2 Golden Delicious apples
2–3 tablespoons olive oil
salt
black pepper, freshly ground
1 tablespoon sugar (or to taste) –for sprinkling
1 tablespoon lemon juice or white wine vinegar

Serve with hot or cold roast pork or duck.

Method
Sprinkle cabbage with enough olive oil to moisten it, season, toss well and let stand, covered, in the refrigerator for $\frac{1}{2}$–1 hour.

To prepare the fruit: take grapes from stems and scoop seeds from black grapes with end of a sterilized bobby pin.

Peel oranges and tangerines and section them, discarding membrane from oranges.

Pare, core and dice the apples. Combine all the fruit in a bowl, sprinkle with sugar to taste, add lemon juice or vinegar and toss well. Cover tightly with plastic wrap and keep in refrigerator.

Watchpoint: if apples are cut up more than 1 hour before serving, they will discolor.

To serve: toss cabbage with fruit and pile in salad bowl.

Cucumber and Bean Salad

2 cucumbers
$\frac{1}{2}$ lb green beans
6 tablespoons vinaigrette dressing
salt and pepper

Serve with escalope of veal or poached salmon.

Method
Peel the cucumbers, cut them in half lengthwise and scoop out the seeds. Cut them into $\frac{1}{2}$ inch slices, blanch them in boiling salted water for 1 minute, drain, refresh and drain again. Trim the beans, cut in 2–3 pieces and cook in boiling salted water for 10–12 minutes or until just tender. Drain, refresh and drain again. Mix the beans and cucumber in a salad bowl and toss with vinaigrette dressing and seasoning to taste.

Cucumber and Tomato salad

Peel 3 cucumbers, dice them, removing seeds. Sprinkle with salt, cover and let stand 30 minutes to draw out the juices (dégorger). Peel 3 tomatoes, cut each into 8 wedges and remove the seeds. Rinse cucumbers, drain thoroughly and combine with the tomato wedges.

Make vinaigrette dressing with 3 tablespoons olive oil, 1 tablespoon white wine, salt and pepper and 1 tablespoon chopped mixed herbs (mint, parsley, chives). Spoon over vegetables and chill.

Basque Salad

2 sweet red peppers
2 tomatoes, peeled and sliced
pinch of sugar
1 long hard roll, cut in $\frac{1}{2}$ inch
 slices (for croûtes)

For dressing
1 teaspoon tomato paste
1 teaspoon paprika
1 clove of garlic, crushed
salt
black pepper, freshly ground
2 tablespoons red wine
 vinegar
6 tablespoons olive oil

Serve with cold ham, cold
·fish such as herring in wine
sauce or with cold roast beef.

Method
Broil the peppers under the
broiler until the skin is charred
all over or spear them on a long
fork and roast them over a gas
flame. Rinse them with cold
water to stop cooking and
peel, core, seed and cut them
in strips.

Sprinkle the tomatoes with
a little sugar and toast the
sliced roll. Place the slices of
roll in the bottom of a shallow
serving dish or on individual
plates.

For the dressing: mix the
tomato paste, paprika, and
garlic with salt, pepper and
vinegar. Whisk in the oil until
the dressing thickens slightly.
Pile the peppers and tomatoes on the slices of roll and
spoon the dressing on top.

*Basque salad is served on
small rounds of toast as an
accompaniment to cold meat
or fish*

Salad composée is ideal for serving with steak or lamb chops

Tourangelle

6–8 small new potatoes
½ lb green beans, cut diagonally
 in 1 inch pieces
1 large tart apple
1 tablespoon chopped parsley
 (for garnish)

For lemon cream dressing
¾ cup heavy cream
¾ cup mayonnaise
grated rind and juice of
 ½ lemon
salt and pepper
pinch of dry mustard

Serve this salad with broiled fish or hot or cold baked ham. One small bunch of celery, cut in sticks, can be substituted for the green beans, if you like.

Method
Cook the potatoes in boiling salted water for 15–20 minutes or until just tender. Cool them, peel and cut in sticks. Cook the beans in boiling salted water for 5–8 minutes or until just tender; drain, refresh and drain again.

 To make the dressing: stir the cream into the mayonnaise. Gradually stir in the grated lemon rind and juice, season with salt, pepper and mustard and thin the dressing with a little boiling water if necessary — it should be thin enough to pour.

 Peel, core and slice the apple, add it to the beans and potato sticks and carefully mix in some of the dressing. Season and pile the salad in a bowl, coat it with the remaining dressing and sprinkle with chopped parsley.

Salad Composée
(Combination Salad)

¾ cup rice
3 medium tomatoes, peeled,
 seeded and cut in strips
1 cup (¼ lb) mushrooms
½ cup ripe olives, pitted
1 tablespoon olive oil
6 tablespoons vinaigrette
 dressing (made with red
 wine instead of vinegar) — see
 page 84

Serve with steak, lamb chops.

Method
Cook the rice in boiling salted water for 12–15 minutes or until just tender and drain it. Rinse with hot water, drain again and spread out on a plate to cool and dry. Trim the mushroom stems level with the caps and sauté them in the olive oil until tender. Mix the rice, tomatoes, mushrooms and olives and moisten with the vinaigrette dressing.

Lyonnaise Salad

4 large potatoes
1 Bermuda or large onion,
 thinly sliced
2 tablespoons olive oil
¼ cup vinaigrette dressing (see
 page 84)
1 dill pickle, sliced
1 tablespoon chopped parsley

Serve with hot or cold roast beef or lamb.

Method
Cook the potatoes in boiling salted water for 15–20 minutes or until tender, drain, peel and slice them. Fry the onion in the olive oil until crisp and brown and arrange the potatoes and onion in layers in a serving dish. Mix the vinaigrette dressing with the pickle and parsley and spoon it over the potatoes.

Spanish Salad

1 Bermuda or large onion,
 sliced and pushed into rings
1 green pepper, cored, seeded
 and cut in rings
2 large tomatoes, peeled and
 sliced
salt and pepper
½ cup vinaigrette dressing
 (made with olive oil and
 white wine vinegar) — see
 page 84
1 tablespoon chopped parsley
1 teaspoon thyme

Serve with roast chicken.

Method
Put the onion in a pan of cold water, bring to a boil, add the green pepper and cook for 1 minute; drain, refresh and drain again.

 Mix the tomatoes, onion and pepper in a salad bowl, season and spoon over the vinaigrette dressing; sprinkle with herbs.

Grape, Melon and Mint Salad

1 large honeydew, cantaloupe, or Persian melon
¾ lb seedless green grapes
about 6 sprigs of fresh mint
pinch of sugar (or to taste)

For dressing
¼ cup white wine vinegar
½ cup olive oil
juice of ½ lemon
salt and pepper

Serve with cold roast chicken.

Method
Cut the melon in half, discard the seeds and scoop out the flesh with a ball cutter. Scrape all remaining flesh from shells and discard.

Take grapes from the stems and add to the melon balls with the mint. Whisk all ingredients together for dressing and mix with the melon balls, grapes and mint. Add sugar to taste. Pile the mixture in the melon shells and chill before serving.

Florentine Salad

1¼ cups rice
2 cups (½ lb) small mushrooms
2½ cups chicken stock
2 tablespoons olive oil
salt and pepper
¾ cup mayonnaise
2 teaspoons chopped fresh fennel or dill

Serve with cold roast veal or chicken.

Method
Put the rice in a pan with the stock, cover and simmer 15–18 minutes until all the stock is absorbed and the rice is just tender. Transfer to a bowl to cool.

Trim the mushroom stems level with the caps, sauté them in the oil for 1 minute and let cool. Add them to the rice with seasoning, stir in the mayonnaise to bind the mixture, season, and pile into a glass bowl or on individual plates. Sprinkle with fennel or dill before serving.

Celery, Potato and Olive Salad

5–6 small new potatoes
bunch of celery, cut in sticks
½ cup ripe olives, halved and pitted
1 dessert apple

For dressing
2 tablespoons tomato sauce or tomato ketchup
3 tablespoons heavy cream
1 tablespoon olive oil
squeeze of lemon juice
salt and pepper
pinch of sugar (or to taste)

Serve with steak, cold ham or tongue.

Method
Cook the potatoes in boiling salted water for 15–20 minutes or until just tender; drain, cool and peel them. Cut them in slices and combine in a bowl with the celery and olives. Wipe the apple with a damp cloth, core and dice it, unpeeled, and add to the potato mixture.

Mix the ingredients for the dressing together, season to taste with salt, pepper and sugar. Mix well with the vegetables and pile in a serving dish.

Vancouver Salad

10–12 scallions, trimmed and finely chopped
3 tomatoes, peeled, seeded and cut in wedges
2 green peppers, cored, seeded, thinly sliced and blanched
1 teaspoon wine vinegar
salt and pepper
pinch of sugar
¼ teaspoon dry mustard
6 tablespoons mayonnaise
1 teaspoon Dijon-style mustard
6 tablespoons sour cream

Serve with broiled salmon or shellfish.

Method
Combine the scallions, tomatoes and peppers in a bowl. Mix the vinegar, salt, pepper, sugar and dry mustard together and stir them into the mayonnaise. Stir the Dijon-style mustard into the sour cream and add it to the mayonnaise. Mix carefully with the vegetables, taste for seasoning, cover and chill at least 2 hours before serving.

Tomato and Orange Salad

2 tomatoes, peeled and thinly sliced
3 oranges
1 teaspoon sugar
¼ cup vinaigrette dressing (see page 84)

Serve with hot or cold ham or roast duck.

Method
Sprinkle the sugar over the tomatoes. Thinly peel the rind from 1 orange, cut the strips into needle-like shreds, blanch in boiling water for 1 minute and drain. Cut the remaining rind and pith from the oranges with a serrated-edge knife and section them, discarding the membrane, or slice them. Arrange the oranges in a serving dish with the tomatoes, spoon over the vinaigrette dressing and scatter the shredded peel on top.

Orange, Celery and Chestnut Salad

2 oranges
small bunch of celery, cut in julienne strips
½ lb chestnuts
1 cup stock
½ cup vinaigrette dressing (see page 84)
½ teaspoon sugar (or to taste)

Serve with game or duck.

Method
Soak the celery in ice water for 30 minutes to make it crisp, then drain thoroughly. Roast the chestnuts to loosen the skins and peel them, then simmer them in stock for 20–30 minutes or until tender and drain them. Cut the peel and pith from the oranges with a serrated-edge knife and slice them. Mix the oranges, celery and chestnuts, toss with vinaigrette dressing and sugar to taste and serve.

Chicken Indienne is served with its rice stuffing and the lightly-spiced sauce spooned over (recipe is on page 92)

A PERFECT PARTY MEAL

Pineapple Gelatin

Chicken Indienne
Tomato and Avocado Salad
or
Veal with Cheese and Ham
Sautéed Potatoes

Choux Pralinés au Chocolat
(Chocolate Praline Cream Puffs)

∽

White wine – Châteauneuf-du-Pape Blanc (Rhône)
or Delaware (New York)

Start a simple dinner with colorful pineapple gelatin, followed by chicken stuffed with rice and spiced with curry, or the popular veal, sandwiched with ham and cheese. End the menu with crisp cream puffs filled with a rich chocolate praline-flavored cream.

A curried dish calls for an equally aromatic white wine that can be served well chilled. The whites of Châteauneuf-du-Pape from France's Rhône district are admirably suited to both entrées and are increasingly available here. An intriguing alternative from our native soil and grapes is the Delaware, probably the finest of traditional East Coast white wines.

TIMETABLE

Day before
Make pineapple gelatin, cover tightly and refrigerate.
Make praline powder for choux puffs.
Make stuffing for chicken, cover and refrigerate.

Morning
Make béchamel sauce for chicken and cover tightly.
Prepare, stuff chicken and keep in refrigerator; make chicken stock.
Scald, peel and scoop out tomatoes for salad, and season; keep in plastic bag in refrigerator; make dressing. Make and bake choux puffs; cool and keep in plastic bag; make chocolate filling and chill.
Prepare veal with cheese and ham ready for cooking.

Assemble ingredients for final cooking from 6:00 for dinner around 8 p.m.

You will find that **cooking times** given in the individual recipes for these dishes have sometimes been adapted in the timetable to help you when cooking and serving this menu as a party meal.

Order of Work
6:00
Set oven at moderate (350°F), if using for chicken.
6:15
Start cooking chicken, cover and bake in oven. (If cooking on top of the stove, start cooking at 6:30.)
Unmold pineapple gelatin, add watercress and keep in refrigerator; make dressing and keep covered.
7:40
Turn chicken.
7:00
Turn chicken.
Fill choux puffs and sprinkle with confectioners' sugar.
7:20
Turn chicken onto its back.
Boil potatoes for sautéed potatoes.
Prepare avocados and complete the salad. Arrange tomatoes on individual plates, spoon over dressing and garnish.
7:45
Take chicken from casserole and keep warm; finish sauce. Carve stuffed chicken, arrange on a platter, spoon over sauce and keep warm.
Heat oil and butter in a large skillet and fry escalopes of veal. Peel and sauté potatoes.
8:00
Serve pineapple gelatin.

Appetizer

Pineapple Gelatin

2 cups pineapple juice
1 can (8½ oz) pineapple chunks, in natural juices, drained
juice of 2 large oranges
1 cup dry white wine or water
1 tablespoon white wine vinegar
2 envelopes gelatin
6 tablespoons water
bunch of watercress (for garnish)

For dressing
½ large package (4 oz) cream cheese
1 cup light cream
salt and pepper

Ring mold (5 cup capacity)

Method
Combine pineapple juice, orange juice, wine or water and vinegar in a large pan.

Measure the combined liquids and, if necessary, add enough water to make 1 quart.

Sprinkle gelatin over 6 tablespoons water and let stand about 5 minutes or until spongy.

Dissolve gelatin over a pan of hot water, stir into pineapple juice mixture and pour about one-third into the dampened mold. Let stand in the refrigerator until set.

Arrange the drained pineapple chunks in the mold and fill with the remaining cool but still liquid pineapple mixture. Cover tightly with plastic wrap and chill at least 2 hours or until firmly set.

To make the dressing: work the cream cheese through a sieve into a bowl and beat in the cream a little at a time.

Season to taste and pour into a sauce boat.

To serve, unmold the gelatin onto a flat platter and fill the center with watercress; serve dressing separately.

Spoon the drained pineapple chunks over a layer of chilled pineapple gelatin mixture, then fill the mold with the remaining liquid gelatin

To release pineapple gelatin from the mold, first dip it in a bowl of hot water

Pineapple gelatin, garnished with watercress, is served with a cheese-flavored dressing

Chicken Indienne

$3\frac{1}{2}$–4 lb roasting chicken
$\frac{1}{2}$ lemon
2 tablespoons butter
2 teaspoons curry powder
1 clove of garlic, crushed
1 cup well-flavored chicken stock (made from bones and giblets but not liver) – see page 21
béchamel sauce, made with
   $1\frac{1}{2}$ tablespoons butter,
   $1\frac{1}{2}$ tablespoons flour,
   1 cup milk (infused with slice of onion,
   6 peppercorns, blade of mace and $\frac{1}{2}$ bay leaf)
$\frac{1}{4}$ cup light cream

For stuffing
1 cup long grain rice
$\frac{1}{4}$ cup butter
1 small onion, finely chopped
$\frac{1}{4}$ lb ham, finely chopped
1 tablespoon chopped parsley
1 teaspoon mixed herbs (oregano, thyme)
salt and pepper
1 egg, beaten to mix

Trussing needle and string

Method

Bone the chicken, removing backbone, ribs and thigh bones only and leaving in the breastbone, leg bones and wing bones (for detailed instructions, see Volume 1).

Boil the rice until just tender and drain.

To make the stuffing: melt the butter in a pan, stir in the onion and cook until soft but not brown. Remove from the heat, and mix with the cooked rice, ham and herbs. Season well and stir in enough beaten egg to bind the mixture.

Lay the chicken on a board,

skin side down, spread it with stuffing, sew it up and truss it, reshaping the bird. Rub the chicken thoroughly with the cut lemon.

In a flameproof casserole heat 2 tablespoons butter and when foaming, add curry powder and crushed garlic. Add chicken, placing it on its back, pour in half the stock, cover casserole tightly and simmer on top of stove for about $1\frac{1}{4}$ hours or bake in a moderate oven (350°F) for $1\frac{1}{2}$ hours or until no pink juice runs out when thigh is pierced with a skewer. Turn chicken from one side to the other and finally on its back during cooking. Add extra stock if the pan looks dry.

Prepare the béchamel sauce and cover with plastic wrap.

Remove the chicken from the casserole and keep it warm. Discard any fat from the pan, pour in remaining stock, boil it well to dissolve the pan juices and mix into the béchamel sauce. Simmer the sauce, stirring frequently, for 2–3 minutes. Stir in the cream and taste for seasoning.

Carve the chicken, discarding the trussing strings. Pile stuffed chicken pieces on a platter, spoon over the sauce and serve with a green salad.

Instructions for trussing a chicken are given on page 99.

Make the rice stuffing, season well and bind with beaten egg. Lay boned chicken on board, ready for stuffing

Carve the cooked chicken and arrange the pieces, stuffed with ham and rice, on a platter

After adding curry-flavored stock and cream to the béchamel sauce, spoon it over the chicken pieces

Alternative entrée

Veal with Cheese and Ham

8 veal escalopes (about 1½ lb)
4 thin slices of Gruyère cheese
4 slices of cooked ham
¼ cup seasoned flour (made
    with ¼ teaspoon salt and
    pinch of pepper)
1 egg, beaten to mix
½ cup dry white breadcrumbs
2 tablespoons oil
2 tablespoons butter

Toothpicks

This veal dish almost certainly originated in Switzerland; Gruyère cheese and ham are typical Swiss ingredients.

Method
If necessary, place the veal escalopes between 2 sheets of wax paper and pound them until thin with a mallet or rolling pin. Trim the edges so they are all even sized. Cut the cheese slices in half and lay a slice of cheese on each escalope. Set a slice of ham on 4 escalopes, trimming the edges of the ham or cheese so they do not overlap the meat. Set the remaining escalopes, cheese side down, on top. Secure with toothpicks, coat with seasoned flour, brush with egg and coat with breadcrumbs, pressing in the crumbs with a metal spatula.

In a skillet heat the oil and butter until foaming and fry the escalopes over moderate heat for 4–5 minutes on each side or until golden and melted cheese holds them together.

Remove the toothpicks and serve with sautéed potatoes.

Accompaniment to Alternative entrée

Sautéed Potatoes

1¼ lb potatoes
2 tablespoons oil
2 tablespoons butter
salt and pepper
2 teaspoons chopped parsley

Method
Scrub the potatoes and boil them, unpeeled, until very tender. Drain, peel and cut them in chunks.

In a large skillet heat the oil and, when it is hot, add the butter. Add the potatoes and sauté them until they are crisp and golden brown, turning them occasionally. The potatoes will quickly absorb all the fat and should toast in the hot pan until they are brown and crisp. Turn them occasionally so they brown on several sides, although it is impossible to brown them evenly.

Take from the heat, sprinkle the potatoes with salt and pepper and add the chopped parsley. Serve them in a very hot dish.

Accompaniment to entrée

Tomato and Avocado Salad

8 medium, even-sized
    tomatoes
2 ripe avocados
juice of ½ lemon
salt and pepper
dash of Tabasco
4–5 tablespoons vinaigrette
    dressing (see page 84)
bunch of watercress
    (for garnish)

Method
Scald and peel the tomatoes; cut a slice from the bottom (not stem end) of each tomato, reserving the slices. Carefully scoop out the seeds and discard. Season the insides well with lemon juice, salt and pepper and Tabasco. Chill.

Halve avocados with a silver or stainless steel knife and discard the seeds. Peel and dice the flesh, sprinkle with salt and pepper and mix with a little vinaigrette dressing.

With a teaspoon, fill tomatoes with avocado, replace lids, arrange tomatoes on individual plates and spoon over remaining dressing. Garnish with a few sprigs of watercress.

Watchpoint: do not prepare avocados more than 1 hour before serving as they will discolor.

Dessert

Choux Pralinés au Chocolat
(Chocolate Praline Cream Puffs)

For choux pastry
$\frac{1}{2}$ cup flour
pinch of salt
$\frac{1}{2}$ cup water
$\frac{1}{4}$ cup butter
3 eggs
2 tablespoons slivered almonds, finely chopped
confectioners' sugar (for sprinkling)

For filling
$\frac{1}{4}$ cup praline powder (see box on page 58)
chocolate pastry cream (made with 1 egg, separated, and 1 egg yolk, 2 tablespoons sugar, $\frac{3}{4}$ tablespoon flour, $\frac{1}{2}$ tablespoon cornstarch, $\frac{3}{4}$ cup milk, vanilla bean to flavor, and 3 squares (3 oz) semisweet chocolate, melted)
1 cup heavy cream, whipped until it holds a soft shape

Pastry bag; $\frac{1}{4}$ and $\frac{1}{2}$ inch plain tubes

Method
Set oven at hot (400°F).

To make choux pastry: sift flour with salt onto a piece of wax paper. Put water and butter into a fairly large saucepan, bring to a boil and when bubbling, draw pan from heat and immediately pour in all the flour. Beat vigorously for a few seconds or until mixture is smooth and pulls away from sides of pan to form a ball. Cool mixture about 5 minutes, then beat in eggs one at a time. If eggs are large, break the last one into a bowl and beat with a fork to mix. Add this slowly to pastry dough to ensure that it remains firm and keeps its shape — all of this last egg may not be needed, depending on the consistency of the dough. Beat dough for 1–2 minutes or until it is glossy and very smooth.

Put dough into pastry bag fitted with the $\frac{1}{2}$ inch plain tube and pipe into balls, set fairly far apart, on a dampened baking sheet. Sprinkle with chopped almonds and bake 10 minutes in heated oven, then raise temperature to moderately hot (425°F) and bake 10–12 minutes longer. When puffs are crisp and firm to the touch, take from oven, prick sides to release steam and transfer to a wire rack to cool.

To make chocolate pastry cream: beat egg yolks with sugar until thick and light. Stir in flour and cornstarch and just enough cold milk to make a smooth paste. Add vanilla bean to remaining milk and scald. Cover and let stand 10–15 minutes to infuse. Stir hot milk into egg mixture, blend, return to pan and stir over gentle heat until boiling.

Watchpoint: make sure pastry cream is smooth before letting it boil. If lumps form as it thickens, take pan from heat and beat until smooth. Do not bring to a boil too quickly or the mixture may curdle before it thickens.

Cook pastry cream gently for 2 minutes, stirring; if too stiff, add a little more milk. Remove vanilla bean. Beat egg white until it holds a stiff peak and fold in a little of the hot pastry cream. Fold this mixture into remaining hot cream. Melt chocolate on a heatproof plate over a pan of hot water. Add to cream and let cool.

When pastry cream is cold, fold in whipped cream and praline powder.

Make a slit in the side of each puff and fill with chocolate praline-flavored cream, using the pastry bag fitted with the $\frac{1}{4}$ inch plain tube. Sprinkle choux puffs with confectioners' sugar before serving.

For choux pralinés, flavor the hot pastry cream mixture with the melted chocolate; let cool before adding whipped cream and praline powder

With a pastry bag and plain tube fill puffs with chocolate praline-flavored cream

Choux pralinés au chocolat are sprinkled with confectioners' sugar for serving

HOW TO COOK GAME

Although game was once a staple food all over North America, most of the game available today is raised specially for the table. Because of strict game laws and limited hunting seasons, most game that is not brought home by the individual hunter is only available in specialty stores and is sold frozen.

Wild turkey, goose, duck, dove, quail, squab, partridge, pheasant and grouse are some of the game bird delicacies available; venison, rabbit and bear are also included here.

This feature gives cooking and serving suggestions for all kinds of prepared game from specialty stores and it may also be helpful both to the hunter who had all the fun of hunting and to the cook who prepares the game for dinner.

Points to remember

The way you like to cook your game is a matter of taste. Some connoisseurs insist that the full flavor of game birds can only be appreciated when the flesh is pink or even rare – snipe, for instance, should 'fly through the kitchen', according to the French. Many people prefer their game birds well done, particularly larger birds like turkey or wild goose. Bear and some furred game like rabbit should always be cooked until well done because they can harbor the same trichinae as pork. Venison can be rare or well done, as you prefer.

Game needs strong seasonings to balance its richness – wine, vinegar, red currant jelly and fruits like apples and dried apricots blend beautifully with it. Sour as well as sweet cream is an excellent addition to sauce. Vegetables, too, should be robust rather than delicate – braised red cabbage, braised celery and chestnuts are favorites.

To be sure that the bird is young – look at the legs and feet; they should be smooth and pliable. In the case of a cock (male) bird, the spurs on the legs should be rounded and short, and the feet and toenails supple. The feathers on the breast and under the wings should be downy and soft, with pointed tips on the long wing feathers (rounded points indicate an older bird); in a young bird, the end tip of the breastbone will be pliable. Roast only young birds as older ones can be so tough that they are inedible. If you suspect a bird is middle-aged or elderly, play safe and braise or cook it in a casserole.

All game and some game birds need to be hung if the flesh is to be tender and well-flavored. (Game from a good poultry man will already be hung and well-flavored.) The length of time for hanging depends on your personal taste and the weather (the warmer the weather, the shorter the hanging time). Game is hung (suspended from a hook) so that the air can circulate around it. Hang the game in a cool, dry place such as a dry cellar, a garage or toolshed. Feathered game is hung from the neck; other game by the hind legs.

Birds have been hung long enough when a small tuft of feathers just above the tail can be pulled out easily; the average time for hanging a pheasant so that it develops a distinctive flavor is 10 days; smaller birds mature in 5–7 days. The hanging time for deer and furred game also depends on its size – a deer (venison) should be kept about 14 days, but small game like rabbit should be eaten within 3–4 days.

The weather has a great effect on the aging of game and in warm or humid conditions game should be prepared for the table and eaten almost at once.

Basic Method for Roasting all Game Birds

1–4 young game birds
   (depending on size)
¼ cup butter or bacon fat
salt and pepper
2–4 slices of bacon
1–2 tablespoons flour (for
   sprinkling)
watercress (for garnish)

For stock
giblets from game bird (except
   liver)
1 carrot, sliced
1 onion, sliced
bouquet garni
few peppercorns

For gravy
1 teaspoon flour
½ cup well-flavored beef stock
   (optional)

Trussing needle and string

If the birds have been bought from a poultry market, they will probably have a slice of fresh pork fat tied over the breast. If so, omit the bacon in the recipe.

Method
To make stock: put giblets in a saucepan, cover with water and add the vegetables, bouquet garni, peppercorns and salt. Cover and simmer 30–40 minutes.

Set oven at temperature indicated for the kind of bird.

Wipe insides of birds with a damp cloth or paper towels. Do not wash them. Put a tablespoon of butter with salt and pepper inside each bird and truss them.

If birds have no fat tied on when you buy them, tie bacon slices over the breasts. Heat remaining butter or bacon fat in a roasting pan, put in the birds and baste well. Roast in heated oven, turning birds and basting often so that thighs and undersides are well browned.

Cooking time varies according to kind of bird.

Test birds by pricking thickest parts of thighs – the juice which runs out should be pink or clear, depending on how rare or well done you like your game.

Five minutes before serving, remove bacon or pork fat, baste the breasts well and sprinkle with flour. Baste again before returning to the oven for the final 5 minutes. This makes the breasts of the birds brown and crisp. Remove birds from oven, discard trussing strings and keep birds hot.

To make gravy: discard fat from roasting pan, leaving sediment. Sprinkle in 1 teaspoon flour and blend it into the pan juices. Cook 2–3 minutes or until flour is brown, then pour in the strained stock mixed with beef stock, if you like, to improve the flavor. Cook until the gravy boils, scraping sides and bottom of pan. Continue cooking 1–2 minutes or until the gravy is well reduced and well flavored. Season to taste and strain. Garnish birds with watercress and serve with gravy and the accompaniments suggested on page 101.

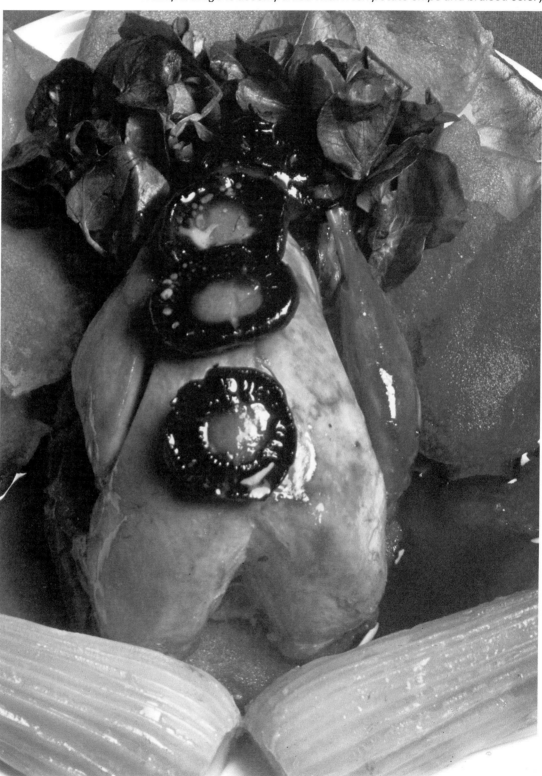

Trussing a bird

The best way to truss a bird is to use string and a special long trussing needle. However, it is quite possible to hold the bird firmly together in the same position by using skewers and tying string around them.

Fold flap of skin over back of neck end, fold ends of wing pinions backwards and under to hold neck skin in position. Place bird on back, press legs down into sides to plump up the breast.

To truss with a needle
1 Thread trussing needle with a strong thread or thin string. Insert needle through wing nearest you, then through thigh and body to emerge in same position on far side.
2 Insert needle again into one end of other wing, then into far end of same joint (leaving a stitch showing 1–2 inches long, depending on size of wing) and pass back through body and out at corresponding part of the first wing.
3 Tie the two thread ends into a bow.
4 Re-thread needle, insert through fleshy skin at end of one drumstick, through the gristle on each side of the pope's nose, and out through skin of other drumstick end.
5 Re-insert needle into carcass under drumsticks; draw through.
6 Tie the two thread ends firmly at side.

To truss with a skewer
Push skewer through bird below thigh bone, turn onto its breast. Catch in the wing pinions, pass string under ends of skewer and cross pinions over its back. Turn bird over, bring up string to secure drumsticks and tie around pope's nose.

Roast pheasant is served with sautéed mushrooms and bacon rolls; and fried breadcrumbs, potato chips, gravy and bread sauce

REGULAR ACCOMPANIMENTS FOR ROAST GAME BIRDS

Fresh Potato Chips

Freshly made potato chips have a totally different flavor from ready prepared ones. Select large potatoes ($1\frac{1}{2}$ lb will serve up to 6 people), peel and trim off the ends. Cut potatoes in very thin even slices on a mandoline slicer (a rectangular piece of wood or metal fitted with plain or fluted sharp blade that can be adjusted according to thickness of slice). Soak slices in a large bowl of ice water for about 1 hour, separating the slices to keep them from sticking together.

Drain well, wrap in a clean dish towel and let stand for 20 minutes, again separating slices so they dry thoroughly.

Fry the slices, a few at a time, in a basket in hot deep fat (350°F on a fat thermometer). When the bubbling subsides, remove them. When all potato slices have been cooked in this way, reheat the fat to 375°F, put some slices in the basket and fry until they are golden brown, separating them when necessary. Drain well on paper towels, pile them into a hot serving dish, sprinkle with salt and serve.

Watchpoint: never cover freshly fried potato chips with a lid or they will lose their crispness.

Game Croûtes

If a small game bird is placed on a thick slice of bread during roasting, the juices from the bird drain into the bread and form a delicious crisp game croûte. The only disadvantage is that the pan juices are not available to make gravy, so a separate gravy must be made.

To make a game croûte: cut crusts from a $\frac{1}{2}-\frac{3}{4}$ inch thick slice of bread. Chop liver of the bird. Melt 1 tablespoon butter in a pan, add 1 shallot or scallion, chopped, and sauté until soft. Add the chopped liver and cook until brown. Season highly with salt and pepper, mash the mixture with a fork and spread it on the bread. Set the bird on top and roast as usual.

Croûtes are not cooked with large birds as the bread would burn during long cooking.

Fried Breadcrumbs

$\frac{3}{4}$ cup fresh white
   breadcrumbs
4 tablespoons butter

Method
Heat butter over low heat, skimming well. Add breadcrumbs and cook, stirring, until they are golden brown. Serve in a small bowl.

Wild Rice

1 cup wild rice
$\frac{1}{4}$ cup butter
1 medium onion, finely chopped
$\frac{1}{2}$ green pepper, finely chopped
salt and pepper

Method
Cook rice, covered, in plenty of boiling salted water for about 40 minutes or until tender but still firm; drain and refresh.

Heat butter in a small skillet, add onion and green pepper and cook for about 5 minutes or until soft but not brown. Combine with the rice, season to taste and reheat well.

Gravy for Game Birds

1 lb chicken giblets (mixed necks and gizzards and any game giblets available, except liver)
$\frac{1}{2}$ lb shank of beef
1 tablespoon beef drippings or oil
1 medium onion, sliced
$3\frac{1}{3}$ cups water, or 3 cups water and $\frac{1}{3}$ cup well-flavored stock
2 teaspoons flour (optional)
bouquet garni
6 peppercorns
1 small carrot, sliced
1 teaspoon salt
1 whole clove

A simple gravy can be made as described in the basic recipe for roasting game birds, but sometimes this is not possible, e.g. when the bird is cooked on a game croûte. Also, large birds often need more gravy than can be made satisfactorily from the pan juices. This recipe makes $2-2\frac{1}{2}$ cups gravy.

Method
Wash and blanch the giblets by putting in cold water, bringing to a boil and draining. Dry giblets and cut them and the beef in small pieces. Melt drippings or oil in a shallow pan, add onion, giblets and beef and cook over low heat until all are lightly browned, shaking pan occasionally to prevent sticking.

Pour in about $\frac{1}{3}$ cup of the water or stock and continue cooking gently, stirring occasionally, until liquid has cooked down to a brown glaze. Stir in flour, if used, and cook 1 minute. Add remaining water and the rest of the ingredients. Bring gravy to a boil, lower heat and simmer with the pan half-covered for 1 hour. Strain the gravy and let stand until cold. Skim off any fat and use as required.

Watchpoint: gentle simmering keeps the gravy glossy and boiling will make it cloudy. If the $\frac{1}{3}$ cup liquid used first is a good stock instead of water, the liquid will reduce to a glaze much more quickly.

Bread Sauce

4–6 tablespoons fresh white breadcrumbs
$1\frac{1}{4}$ cups milk
1 small onion, stuck with 2 cloves
$\frac{1}{2}$ bay leaf
salt and pepper
2 tablespoons butter

Method
Bring milk to a boil, add onion and bay leaf, cover the pan and let it stand on side of stove (not over heat) for about 15 minutes to infuse. Remove onion and bay leaf and discard, add breadcrumbs and seasoning and return to heat. Stir the sauce gently until it comes to a boil. Beat in the butter, a little at a time, and serve hot.

Broiled Hominy Squares

1 cup coarse hominy grits
1 teaspoon salt
½ cup grated Parmesan cheese
3 tablespoons butter

9 inch square cake pan

Method

Bring 3 cups water to a rolling boil. Combine hominy with 1 cup cold water and salt. Stir into boiling water and cook, stirring, for about 15 minutes or until very thick. Pour into the pan and let cool until firm.

Cut hominy into 1½–2 inch squares and place in a shallow baking dish. Sprinkle squares with Parmesan cheese, dot with butter and broil about 4 inches from broiling unit for 4–5 minutes or until brown. Serve hot.

Buttered Turnips

1 large rutabaga or other
   yellow turnip
1 medium potato
2–3 tablespoons butter
salt and pepper
1½–2 cups half and half,
   warmed until hot

Method

Peel turnip and potato, cut in even-sized pieces and cook in boiling salted water for 15–20 minutes or until tender when tested with the tip of a knife. Drain, return to the pan and cook a few minutes over low heat until dry. Take from heat, add butter with seasoning to taste and mash with a potato masher or fork until smooth. Beat in half and half. If preparing ahead, beat in only 1 cup half and half and pour over the remainder. Do not stir but replace lid and keep pan in a warm place for

up to 30 minutes. Turnips will absorb liquid on standing.

Just before serving, beat the turnips over the heat with a wooden spoon until smooth, adding extra hot half and half if necessary.

Sauerkraut Salad

1 medium can (1 lb) sauerkraut
1 green pepper, finely chopped
1 small onion, finely chopped
2 stalks of celery, finely
   chopped
1 cup chili sauce
⅓ cup brown sugar
3 tablespoons lemon juice

Method

Drain sauerkraut thoroughly and place in a salad bowl. Stir in green pepper, onion and celery. Combine chili sauce, brown sugar and lemon juice. Pour onto salad and toss well.

Orange Salad

3 navel oranges
peeled rind of ½ orange
6 tablespoons vinaigrette
   dressing (see page 84)

Method

Cut peeled orange rind into fine strips, blanch in boiling water for 5 minutes, drain and reserve.

Cut rind and pith from the navel oranges with a serrated-edge knife and cut out the orange sections. Arrange these in a dish, spoon over the vinaigrette dressing and sprinkle the strips of rind on top. Chill before serving.

GAME BIRDS

Pheasant

Pheasants were introduced to Europe centuries ago from Asia and were brought here by the early settlers. Today wild pheasant is found only in some parts of the country and, since the season is short to protect the game, pheasant has become a luxury food for special occasions.

Young birds may be rotisserie or oven roasted; cocks and slightly older birds should be pot roasted to keep them as moist as possible.

Pheasant lends itself to a variety of dishes, but if served simply roasted, it must be well hung, otherwise it can be dull and tasteless. A large plump bird serves 3–4 people.

Roast according to basic method for 45–55 minutes in a hot oven (400°F). Hen birds are smaller than cocks but they have more flavor and are less dry. Serve with Brussels sprouts or braised celery, sautéed mushrooms, fried breadcrumbs, bread sauce and fresh potato chips.

Roast Pheasant with Truffles

1 large or 2 small pheasant
salt and pepper
2 thin slices of fresh pork fat
   (for larding)
6 tablespoons butter
2 medium truffles, sliced
1 cup stock
kneaded butter (made with 1½
   tablespoons butter and 2
   teaspoons flour)
¾ cup Madeira
¼ cup brandy

Trussing needle and string

Method

Set oven at hot (400°F).

Truss pheasant and rub the skin with a little salt. Cover breast of bird with slices of pork fat. In a casserole heat 3 tablespoons butter, add pheasant and roast, uncovered, in heated oven for 40 minutes or until almost tender, basting often. Remove bird and discard the pork fat and trussing string. Heat remaining butter in a small pan, add truffles and sauté 1–2 minutes. Pour off fat from the casserole and discard it, leaving the sediment. Add stock, bring to a boil and cook, stirring, until the pot juices have dissolved. Thicken them by stirring a little kneaded butter into the hot liquid and bring it to a boil.

Add the Madeira, brandy and truffles, put back the pheasant and baste it with the sauce. Cover casserole and continue cooking for 15 minutes. Transfer pheasant to a warm platter, taste the sauce for seasoning and serve separately with wild rice.

Braised Pheasant Vallée d'Auge

1 large or 2 small pheasant
3 tablespoons butter
1 medium onion, finely sliced
2–3 stalks of celery, sliced
2 medium tart or dessert
   apples, pared, cored and
   sliced
1 tablespoon flour
$\frac{3}{4}$ cup white wine
$1\frac{1}{2}$–2 cups well-flavored stock
salt and pepper
$\frac{1}{2}$ cup heavy cream
1 tablespoon chopped parsley
   (optional)

For garnish
1 bunch of celery
1 green pepper, cored, seeded,
   cut into rings and blanched,
   or 1 slice of canned pimiento,
   drained and cut into rings
2 dessert apples
2 tablespoons butter
granulated sugar (for
   sprinkling)

Trussing needle and string

Method

Set oven at moderate (350°F). Truss the birds.

In a flameproof casserole heat butter and brown birds slowly on all sides. When browned, remove from the casserole and add onion, celery and apples. Sauté over low heat for 5 minutes or until they are soft. Stir in the flour off the heat and add wine and stock. Bring to a boil, season and pour into a bowl. Return pheasants to casserole and pour sauce over them; cover with foil, then the lid and cook in heated oven for 45 minutes or until tender when tested with a fork.

To prepare garnish: cut celery stalks into 2–2$\frac{1}{2}$ inch sticks, tie sticks into bundles with string and cook in boiling salted water for 15–18 minutes. Remove the string and put a ring of blanched pepper or pimiento around each bundle; keep hot.

Wipe the skins of the 2 apples with a damp cloth, core them, cut them into rings $\frac{1}{4}$–$\frac{1}{2}$ inch thick. Melt the butter and fry apple rings over high heat on each side for 1$\frac{1}{2}$–2 minutes, sprinkling lightly with sugar so they brown well. Lift carefully onto a greased plate; keep hot.

Watchpoint: if rings are over-cooked, they become wrinkled and look unattractive.

When birds are tender, take them from the casserole and remove trussing strings. If large, carve pheasant like a chicken; if small, split in half with poultry shears, discarding the backbone. Transfer the bird to a warm platter and keep hot. Strain the sauce, working as much vegetable and apple mixture through strainer as possible. Pour into a saucepan, adjust seasoning, bring to a boil and simmer until glossy and slightly thickened. Add cream and bring just back to a boil. Spoon a little over the birds to coat them and serve the rest separately. Garnish the platter with celery bundles and apple rings. Sprinkle the pheasant with parsley, if you like, and serve with château potatoes.

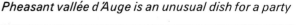

Pheasant vallée d'Auge is an unusual dish for a party

Sprinkle apple slices with sugar for pheasant vallée d'Auge

Garnish the platter with celery bundles and apple rings

Casserole of partridge – spoon a little sauce with sausages over the birds and garnish with watercress

Partridge

No partridge are native to North America so the name partridge is used to cover a variety of wild fowl. This can include both quail or grouse, depending on the part of the country in which you live, as well as European partridge which is specially reared. Most partridge and pheasant recipes are interchangeable. Allow $\frac{1}{2}-\frac{3}{4}$ bird per person, depending on size.

Roast according to basic method for 20–25 minutes in a hot oven (425°F). Serve with bread sauce, broiled mushrooms and regular or Savoy cole slaw.

Casserole of Partridge

2–3 plump partridges
1½–2 cups stock (made from carcasses, 1 onion, 1 carrot, bouquet garni, 6 peppercorns, little salt)
2–3 tablespoons butter
6–8 ($\frac{1}{2}-\frac{3}{4}$ lb) country sausages
1 onion, sliced
1 carrot, sliced
2 slices of bacon, blanched and diced
2 teaspoons flour
bouquet garni
4–6 slices of bread, crusts removed and fried in oil and butter (mixed) – for croûtes

For stuffing
1 cup fresh white breadcrumbs
$\frac{1}{4}$ cup raisins
$\frac{1}{4}$ cup chopped walnuts
1 shallot, finely chopped
2 tablespoons butter
1 teaspoon finely chopped parsley
1 egg, beaten to mix
salt and pepper

Trussing needle and string, or poultry pins

Method
Set oven at moderately low (325°F).

Bone the partridges as for pheasant, leaving in the leg and wing bones (see Volume 10 for instructions).

Wipe the carcasses, break them up and put in a saucepan with ingredients for stock and water to cover. Partly cover the pan and simmer 1–1½ hours or until stock is strong. Strain and measure 1½–2 cups.

To prepare stuffing: cook shallot in butter until soft but not brown and mix with the remaining ingredients. Stir in the egg to bind the mixture and season to taste. Lay out birds, spread stuffing on them, reshape and sew up with string or secure with poultry pins.

Heat butter in a flameproof casserole, put in the sausages and brown over a low heat. Remove them, add partridges and brown on all sides. Add the onion, carrot and bacon and cook 2–3 minutes. Sprinkle with flour, add bouquet garni and the measured stock. Cover casserole tightly and cook in heated oven for 45–60 minutes or until the birds are tender.

Remove partridges from the casserole, discard trussing strings and cut birds in half. Transfer them to a warm platter and serve each half on a croûte of bread. Cut sausages in half diagonally and add to casserole. Remove bouquet garni and spoon a little of the sauce and some of the sausages over the partridges; serve the rest separately. Garnish with watercress. Braised red cabbage is a good accompaniment.

Braised Red Cabbage

This is even better cooked the day before and reheated thoroughly before serving.

Blanch 1 medium head of red cabbage (shredded) in kettle of boiling water for 1 minute; drain. (It will turn deep violet but when vinegar is added it will return to its original color.)

In a flameproof casserole melt 2 tablespoons butter and fry 1 sliced onion until soft but not brown. Add 2 tart apples (pared, cored and sliced) and cook 2–3 minutes longer; remove from the pan. Add the cabbage in layers with the apple mixture, sprinkling with 2–3 tablespoons wine vinegar, 1½ tablespoons sugar, salt, pepper and 2–3 tablespoons water. Cover with buttered brown paper and lid and braise in a moderately low oven (325°F) for 1½–2 hours or until the cabbage is very tender. Stir it occasionally and moisten with a little extra water if necessary.

Stir in the kneaded butter (made with 2 tablespoons butter and 1 tablespoon flour) a little at a time, adding just enough to thicken the cabbage juices slightly. Adjust seasoning.

Partridge with Black Olives

2–3 plump partridges
½ cup black olives, halved and pitted
3–4 tablespoons butter
4–6 oz salt pork, diced
3 shallots, finely chopped
1 tablespoon flour
1 teaspoon tomato paste
1½ cups well-flavored stock
1 cup red wine
salt and pepper
bouquet garni

Trussing needle and string

Method
Set oven at moderate (350°F). Truss the birds.

In a deep flameproof casserole heat the butter and brown the birds slowly on all sides. Blanch the salt pork and drain. Add it to the partridges with the shallots and fry gently 3–4 minutes longer. Remove birds.

Stir flour into casserole, add tomato paste and stock. In a separate saucepan boil the wine until it is reduced by one-third and add to the casserole. Bring to a boil, season, add the bouquet garni and replace the partridges.

Cover the casserole with a piece of foil and then the lid. Bake in heated oven for 50–60 minutes or until birds are tender when tested with a fork. Remove them, discard trussing strings, split birds in half and trim away the backbone.

Transfer the birds to a warm platter, boil the sauce rapidly for 2–3 minutes or until it is glossy and slightly thick and strain it into a saucepan. Stir in the black olives, reboil, taste for seasoning and spoon the sauce over the birds.

Squab, Pigeon and Dove

Squabs are young pigeons that do not fly and, because they are always tender and have a distinctive flavor, they are a real delicacy. Wood pigeon and dove are usually interchangeable in recipes, but can be tough even when cooked slowly in a casserole, so only young squabs are popular. Serve 1 pigeon or squab per person unless pigeon is large, when it is split in half. For doves, allow ½–¾ bird per person, depending on size.

Roast squab and pigeon according to basic method for 30–45 minutes (depending on size) in a moderate oven (350°F). Serve on fried hominy squares or with wild rice and sauerkraut salad.

Roast dove according to basic method for 20–25 minutes in a hot oven (425°F). Cook on a croûte of bread. Good with broiled bananas.

St. Hubert is the patron saint of hunters. He was converted to Christianity when he was hunting on a Good Friday and saw a vision of the Crucifix between the horns of the stag he was about to kill.

Roast Squabs St. Hubert

3–4 squabs
6–7 tablespoons butter
1 cup red wine
½ cup veal or game stock
1 tablespoon red currant jelly
¼ cup blanched almonds or cashews

For pilaf
1 cup rice
½ cup dried apricots
2–3 dried apple rings
1 medium onion, finely chopped
3 tablespoons butter
2 cups veal or game stock
salt and pepper

Trussing needle and string

Method
Soak apricots and apple rings, if necessary, according to package directions. Set oven at moderately hot (375°F).

Truss the squabs; rub with 3–4 tablespoons butter, put in a roasting pan and pour in ½ cup red wine. Roast in heated oven, basting often, for 35–40 minutes or until tender. Increase heat to hot (400°F), if necessary, during last 5 minutes so squabs brown well.

To prepare dried fruit: cook apples and apricots in water to cover for 10–15 minutes or until tender. Drain and, when cool enough to handle, cut in pieces.

To prepare pilaf: cook onion in 2 tablespoons butter in a flameproof casserole until lightly browned. Stir in the rice, add the stock, season and bring to a boil. Cover and bake in the oven with the squabs for about 12 minutes.

With a fork stir cooled fruit into the rice. Season well and dot the top with 1 tablespoon butter. Cover with foil and the lid and bake 10 minutes,

or until rice is tender, stirring once or twice with a fork.

Take squabs from pan, remove trussing strings, split them and trim away the backbone. Pour any fat from the roasting pan and discard. Dissolve juices with remaining ½ cup red wine and ½ cup stock. Stir in red currant jelly and boil hard for 1 minute; season and strain. Split nuts in half and fry in remaining butter until brown.

Pile pilaf down the center of a warm platter; arrange squabs around it. Spoon a little gravy over squabs and serve the rest separately. Sprinkle browned nuts over the dish and serve.

For squabs St. Hubert, mix the cooked apricots and apples into the rice for pilaf

Squabs St. Hubert are arranged around pilaf and scattered with browned nuts for serving

Squabs en Cocotte Normande

4 squabs
3 tablespoons butter
2–3 shallots, finely chopped
2 tablespoons Calvados, or applejack
1–1½ cups well-flavored stock
2 dessert apples, pared, cored and sliced
bouquet garni
salt and pepper
kneaded butter (made with 1 tablespoon butter and ½ tablespoon flour)
½ cup heavy cream
1 tablespoon chopped parsley

Trussing needle and string

Method
Truss the squabs. In a flameproof casserole, heat butter, put in the birds and brown slowly on all sides. Add the shallots and continue to cook slowly for 3 minutes longer, turning the birds occasionally.

Heat the Calvados or applejack, flame and pour it, flaming, into the casserole. Add 1 cup stock, apples, bouquet garni and seasoning. Bring to a boil and cook gently on top of the stove for ½ hour or until birds are tender when tested with a fork.

Watchpoint: if the liquid in the pan evaporates too fast, add a little extra stock during cooking.

Remove squabs from the casserole and discard the trussing strings. Transfer squabs to a warm platter and keep warm.

Remove bouquet garni and work mixture in the casserole through a strainer. Return mixture to the casserole, bring to a boil and thicken very slightly by whisking in a little kneaded butter. Add the cream, simmer 1–2 min-

utes, taste for seasoning, spoon sauce over birds and sprinkle generously with chopped parsley. Serve with château potatoes.

Casserole of Dove or Pigeon

4 young doves or pigeons
6 tablespoons oil
salt and pepper
2 small onions, finely chopped
1 clove of garlic, finely chopped
1 green pepper, cored, seeded and cut in thin strips
2½ cups stock
1 cup rice
⅓ cup pine nuts or chopped walnuts
1 cup (¼ lb) mushrooms, sliced
3 slices of pimiento, drained and cut in thin strips
1 teaspoon paprika

Trussing needle and string

Method
Set oven at moderate (350°F). Truss the birds.

In a flameproof casserole brown the birds on all sides in 4 tablespoons of the oil. Sprinkle with salt and pepper, add onions, garlic, green pepper and ½ cup stock. Cover the casserole tightly and bake in heated oven for 20 minutes.

In a skillet heat remaining oil, add rice and cook, stirring frequently, until it is lightly browned. Add to the casserole with nuts, mushrooms, pimiento and paprika. Add remaining stock. Replace casserole in the oven, without a cover, and bake 20 minutes or until the rice is tender and the liquid has been completely absorbed. Remove trussing strings before serving.

Wild Duck

Wild duck has dark, rich delicious meat. Similar to domestic duck but with a flavor all its own, wild duck comes in various sizes and there are many kinds. Wild duck blends well with the same flavors that complement domestic duck — oranges, apples, rice and good wine. One wild duck usually serves 2 people, depending on size, but sometimes they are so small that 2 are enough for only 1 portion.

Roast according to basic method for 30–35 minutes in a hot oven (400°F) for an average bird serving 2 people. Serve with watercress, gravy, fried breadcrumbs, fresh potato chips and orange salad.

Roast Wild Duck with Orange Gravy

2 wild ducks
¼ cup butter
salt and pepper
3–4 slices of bacon
little flour (for sprinkling)
watercress (for garnish)

For orange gravy
3–4 strips of orange rind
juice of 1 orange
1 tablespoon butter
1 small onion, sliced
1 cup well-flavored stock
¼ cup port or red wine
pinch of cayenne
black pepper, freshly ground
1 teaspoon arrowroot (mixed to a paste with 1 tablespoon water) – optional

Trussing needle and string

Method
Set oven at hot (400°F).

Put 1 tablespoon butter, mixed with salt and pepper,

inside each duck and truss them. Lay bacon slices over the breasts. Heat remaining butter in the roasting pan, put in ducks and baste with hot butter.

Roast ducks in heated oven, basting frequently, for 30–35 minutes or until they are tender. Just before the end of cooking, remove bacon slices from the ducks, sprinkle the breasts with flour, baste well and cook 5 minutes longer.

For gravy: in a pan heat butter and fry the onion until golden. Add the orange rind and stock, simmer 10 minutes and strain. Return liquid to the pan, add the strained orange juice, port or wine, cayenne, salt and black pepper. Bring to a boil and, if you like, stir in a little arrowroot paste to thicken the mixture slightly.

Transfer ducks to a warm platter, remove the trussing strings, garnish with watercress and serve the gravy separately. Orange salad and château potatoes are good accompaniments.

Another recipe for duck with orange is given on page 32.

Roast wild duck with orange gravy is garnished with watercress

Pot Roast Wild Duck with Sour Cream

2 wild ducks
$\frac{1}{4}$ cup seasoned flour (made with $\frac{1}{4}$ teaspoon salt and pinch of pepper)
2 tablespoons butter
1 onion, chopped
2 tablespoon chopped parsley
1 teaspoon rosemary
1 teaspoon thyme
1 cup red wine
1 cup sour cream
salt and pepper

Trussing needle and string

Method
Set oven at moderate (350°F). Truss ducks.

Coat ducks in seasoned flour. Melt butter in a deep flameproof casserole and brown the ducks on all sides. Add the onion, herbs and red wine, cover and pot roast in heated oven for 1 hour or until the ducks are tender. Transfer the ducks to a warm platter and remove the trussing strings.

Add sour cream to the pan and reheat sauce without boiling. Taste for seasoning, spoon over ducks and serve.

Wild Turkey

Wild turkey is not as rare as it used to be. It differs from domestic turkey in shape, size and flavor and, unlike some other game birds, it has a juicy flesh. Wild turkey should be prepared simply. Allow 1 lb turkey per person.

Roast small birds according to basic method for 20 minutes per lb; for medium birds – 18 minutes per lb; for large birds – 16 minutes per lb, in a moderate oven (350°F). Traditional accompaniments are cranberry sauce, buttered squash or turnips; boiled onions.

Braised Wild Turkey

1 small wild turkey
$\frac{1}{2}$ cup butter
2 onions, sliced
2 carrots, sliced
2 stalks of celery, sliced
large bouquet garni
1 quart well-flavored stock
1 tablespoon arrowroot (mixed to a paste with 2 tablespoons water)
salt and pepper

Trussing needle and string
Method
Set oven at moderately hot (375°F). Truss the turkey.

In a large flameproof casserole, melt the butter and brown the turkey on all sides over fairly low heat. Remove it, add vegetables, lower heat, cover the pan and cook 5–7 minutes. Put back the turkey, add bouquet garni and half the stock, cover the pan and braise in heated oven for 2–3 hours or until the bird is very tender. Add more stock to the pan during cooking if it gets dry.

Take turkey from the pan and remove trussing strings. Transfer it to a warm platter and keep warm.

Strain the juice from the pan, skim off any fat and add the remaining stock. Boil to reduce the gravy to about 2 cups, then stir a little arrowroot paste into the hot gravy to thicken it slightly. Season to taste, spoon a little over the turkey and serve the rest separately.

The traditional accompaniments are stuffing balls, baked or fried in butter, cranberry sauce and wild rice or corn fritters.

Stuffing Balls

2 tablespoons melted butter
1 cup fresh white breadcrumbs
salt and pepper
1 tablespoon chopped parsley
1 teaspoon mixed herbs (oregano, thyme, marjoram)
1 small egg, beaten to mix

Method
Sprinkle butter over crumbs, season well, add herbs and bind the mixture together with beaten egg. Roll mixture into small balls the size of walnuts. Fry in 2 tablespoons butter or bake in a moderate oven (350°F) for 20–25 minutes or until brown.

Wild Goose

Wild goose is a rarity unless you know a hunter but if you are lucky enough to be offered one, you will find the meat rich and dark with an excellent flavor. If you plan to roast it, be sure the goose is young because old geese are very, very tough. Allow 1 lb goose per person.

Roast according to basic method for 15 minutes per lb in a hot oven (400°F). Baste goose frequently with white wine and serve with wild rice and buttered turnips.

Roast Wild Goose with Mushroom Cream Sauce

5–6 lb wild goose
$\frac{1}{2}$ cup butter
salt and pepper
$\frac{1}{2}$ cup white wine
watercress (for garnish)

For mushroom cream sauce
$\frac{1}{2}$ cup (2 oz) sliced mushrooms
3 tablespoons goose fat (from roasting goose)
1 medium onion, finely chopped
1 goose liver, chopped
1 cup well-flavored stock
1 cup light cream
2 egg yolks, lightly beaten
2 tablespoons brandy
2 tablespoons chopped parsley

Trussing needle and string

Method
Set oven at hot (400°F).

Put 2 tablespoons butter mixed with salt and pepper inside the goose and truss it. Melt remaining butter in a roasting pan, place goose on rack in pan, add wine, baste well and roast in heated oven, allowing 15 minutes per lb; baste goose frequently. Season outside with salt and pepper near the end of roasting time.

To make sauce: pour 3 tablespoons fat from the roasting pan into a saucepan and fry onion in it until lightly browned. Add the goose liver and mushrooms and continue cooking for about 5 minutes. Stir in 1 cup stock and simmer 3–4 minutes. Add a little hot sauce to cream, mixed with the egg yolks, return to pan and cook over low heat, stirring constantly, until sauce thickens. Do not let it boil. Stir in the brandy and parsley and season to taste.

Transfer goose to a warm platter, remove trussing strings and garnish with watercress. Serve the sauce separately and accompany goose with wild rice and buttered turnips or squash.

Quail

There are many varieties of quail but they only differ slightly in size and flavor.

There are two schools of thought about cleaning quail; some cooks insist they should not be drawn (that is, intestines are left inside), while others draw them. Quail should be eaten fresh and they are at their best when roasted, with constant basting to keep them moist. They can also be stuffed or cooked like partridge, with which they are sometimes confused. Quail are small birds and 1 bird will serve 1 person.

Roast according to basic method for 20 minutes in a very hot oven (450°F). Serve on buttered toast or cook on a croûte of bread. Wild rice and salad of watercress sprinkled with lemon juice are good accompaniments. Serve cold quail with Cumberland sauce.

Quail with Raisins

4 quail
8 slices of bacon, cut in short strips
3–4 tablespoons butter
salt and pepper
1½–2 cups brown stock
16 small onions
1 teaspoon sugar (for sprinkling)
½ cup seedless raisins

Trussing needle and strings

Method
Truss the quail. Blanch the bacon by putting in a pan of cold water, bringing to a boil and draining. In a casserole melt the butter and fry the bacon until crisp. Take out bacon and reserve. Add the quail to the pan and brown slowly on all sides. Drain any excess fat. Add the bacon, season with salt and pepper and pour in stock. Bring to a boil, cover tightly and bake in a moderately low oven (325°F) for 30–40 minutes or until very tender.

Sauté the onions in the casserole, adding a sprinkling of sugar to help them brown. Add to the casserole after quail have cooked 20 minutes before serving. At the end of cooking, the gravy should be well reduced, brown and sticky.

Watchpoint: to make good gravy, jellied stock is essential, otherwise it will need thickening with kneaded butter or arrowroot.

Serve with chestnut purée or Parisienne potatoes.

Chestnut Purée

2 lb chestnuts, peeled
1 stalk of celery
bouquet garni
2 cups stock
¼ cup butter
¼ teaspoon allspice
salt and pepper

This purée is delicious with game or pork.

Method
In a saucepan cook chestnuts with celery, bouquet garni and stock until boiling; cover and simmer 45 minutes or until the chestnuts are very tender but not mushy. Drain them, discard the celery and bouquet garni and work chestnuts through a sieve or food mill, or purée in a blender with a little cooking liquid.

Return purée to the pan and beat in the butter over heat. Season with allspice and salt and pepper to taste. The purée should be light and not at all sticky. If too thick, beat in a little of the cooking liquid.

Parisienne Potatoes

5–6 large potatoes, peeled
¼ cup butter
salt

Method
Scoop out balls from the potatoes with a ball cutter.

In a skillet melt the butter and sauté the potatoes over medium heat for 10–15 minutes or until tender, shaking the pan so the balls brown evenly. Sprinkle them with a little salt just before serving.

Stuffed Quail en Cocotte Alsacienne

4 plump quail
3—4 tablespoons butter
¼ cup sherry
½ cup stock
bouquet garni
2—3 stalks of celery, sliced

For stuffing
1 medium onion, finely chopped
1 tablespoon butter
½ lb ground pork
2 tablespoons fresh white
   breadcrumbs
1 teaspoon sage
salt and pepper
1 egg yolk

For sauce
2—3 tart apples, pared, cored
   and sliced
1 tablespoon butter
sugar (to taste)
2—3 tablespoons cider
½ cup heavy cream
2 teaspoons arrowroot (mixed
   to a paste with 1½
   tablespoons water)

Trussing needle and string

Method
Set oven at moderate (350°F).

To prepare stuffing: cook onion in butter until it is soft but not brown. Add onion to the pork, breadcrumbs and sage. Season and mix stuffing with egg yolk to bind it. Fill quail with the stuffing and truss them.

Heat the butter in a flame-proof casserole and carefully brown the quail on all sides. Add sherry and flame it. Add stock, bouquet garni and celery. Cover tightly and bake in heated oven or simmer on top of the stove for 25—30 minutes or until birds are tender.

To prepare sauce: cook apples to a pulp with the butter over a low heat. Work the mixture through a strainer and return it to the pan. Season, add sugar to taste and stir in the cider. Simmer 5 minutes.

Take quail from casserole and remove trussing strings; transfer them to a warm platter. Strain cooking liquid and add to the apple sauce. Stir in the cream and a little arrowroot paste to thicken the mixture slightly. Bring sauce just to a boil. Spoon some over the quail and serve the rest separately.

Woodcock and Snipe

Woodcock and snipe — small birds prized by gourmets — are difficult to find. They are usually broiled or roasted and cooked undrawn (with the intestines left inside). One bird will serve 1 person.
Roast according to basic method for 12—15 minutes in a very hot oven (450°F). Cook on a croûte of bread and serve with fresh potato chips and orange salad.

Grouse

Grouse are usually the size of a small chicken but they have dark brown feathers. The meat, which tastes best broiled or roasted, is dark and rich and does not need a sauce.

One bird will serve 1—2 people (or 2 large ones will serve 4), depending on size. Old grouse, which tend to be tough, need long cooking in a casserole.

Roast according to basic method for 30—35 minutes in a hot oven (400°F). Serve half a bird on a game croûte with fresh potato chips, green salad and cranberry or bread sauce.

Grouse and Beef Pie

2 grouse
2 lb flank steak
3 lambs' kidneys
2 cup quantity of rich pie
   pastry (see Volume 1)
stuffing balls (see box on
   page 110)
1 small onion, finely chopped
½ lb bacon, blanched and diced
1 cup (¼ lb) chopped
   mushrooms
salt and pepper
1 cup stock (made from grouse
   bones, 1 onion, 1 carrot,
   few peppercorns, little salt)
beaten egg (for glaze)

*Deep pie dish (8—9 inch
   diameter)*

This pie can be made with any game bird or with venison. Serves 6—8.

Method
Make pastry dough and chill. Set oven at hot (400°F).

Cut grouse meat from bones and cut into strips, discarding skin, and make stock with bones. Skin kidneys and cut in half lengthwise.

Arrange grouse, steak, onion, bacon, kidneys and mushrooms in layers in the pie dish. Season well and put stuffing balls on top. Pour in the stock. Roll out pastry, cover pie, trim around edge, make a hole in center of pie to allow steam to escape and decorate with pastry cutouts made from trimmings.

Brush with beaten egg to glaze. Bake in heated oven for 25—30 minutes or until pastry is brown, then wrap pie dish in foil. Lower oven heat to moderate (350°F) and bake 1½ hours longer or until meat is very tender when tested with a skewer through hole in center of pastry. Serve hot or cold.

OTHER GAME

Bear

Enthusiasts insist that the delicate diet of bears — vegetables, berries, honey — gives the meat its excellent flavor. When hung and marinated, it can be treated like beef, but it is too tough and dry to roast.

The best cuts are the saddle, loin, haunch or ribs, but avoid neck and hindquarters of the bear as they are tough. Trim all fat before marinating because it turns rancid quickly and gives the meat a bad taste.

Bear Ardennaise

$2\frac{1}{2}$–3 lb bear steak, cut from the loin
$\frac{1}{4}$ lb salt pork, cut in $\frac{1}{4}$ inch strips (for larding)
1 tablespoon oil
3 large onions, thinly sliced
$1\frac{1}{2}$ cups ale
$1\frac{1}{2}$ cups stock
1 clove of garlic, crushed with $\frac{1}{2}$ teaspoon salt
1 teaspoon red wine vinegar
1 teaspoon sugar
bouquet garni
black pepper, freshly ground
2 teaspoons Dijon-style mustard
1 tablespoon heavy cream
1 tablespoon flour
salt and pepper
1 can (16 oz) unsweetened chestnut purée
1 tablespoon butter

For marinade
$\frac{1}{4}$ cup oil
$\frac{1}{2}$ cup red wine
$\frac{1}{2}$ cup red wine vinegar
2 bay leaves
1 onion, sliced
1 carrot, sliced

Larding needle

Method

Lard one side of the bear steak with the salt pork, combine ingredients for the marinade, pour over the steak, cover and refrigerate 1–3 days, turning occasionally; drain.

Set oven at moderate (325°F).

In a heavy flameproof casserole, heat oil and slowly brown the onions. When they are well browned, place the bear steak on top, larded side up, pour in the ale and stock and add the garlic, vinegar, sugar and bouquet garni. Season well with black pepper, cover the pan and bake in heated oven for about $2\frac{1}{2}$ hours or until the meat is tender. (An older animal will need to cook $3\frac{1}{2}$–4 hours.) Remove the lid of the pan, baste the meat and continue cooking, uncovered, for 15 minutes longer. Remove meat from the pan and transfer to a baking sheet. Mix mustard and cream together, spread it over the surface of the meat and return to the oven until tips of lardons are crisp.

Strain the cooking liquid, reserving the onions. Skim off all the fat and mix about 2 tablespoons with 1 tablespoon flour. Stir the flour and fat mixture back into the cooking liquid and bring to a boil, stirring, until it thickens. Season to taste.

Heat the chestnut purée, add the reserved onions, season well and stir in the butter. Spoon this down the center of a warm serving dish. Slice the bear steak, arrange it on top and spoon over the gravy. Serve with celeriac croquettes if you like.

Celeriac Croquettes

1 medium head of celeriac or root celery
$\frac{1}{4}$ cup seasoned flour (made with $\frac{1}{4}$ teaspoon salt and pinch of pepper)
1 egg, beaten to mix
$\frac{1}{2}$ cup dry white breadcrumbs
butter (for frying)

Method

Peel the celeriac and cut into wedge-shaped pieces. Simmer in salted water until barely tender. Drain well, leave until cool, then roll in seasoned flour, brush with beaten egg and coat well with breadcrumbs. Fry in butter until golden brown.

Venison

Venison must be hung 2–3 weeks to bring out its exceptional flavor. Many recipes recommend marinating venison any time from 1 hour to several days to improve both the texture and the flavor of the meat.

The best cuts of venison are the saddle and leg. Only the haunch or saddle from very young deer are suitable for roasting; other pieces, such as cuts from the shoulder, are best used in pot roasts, stews and as ground meat.

Game, Steak and Mushroom Pie

1 lb venison or any boneless game, cut in 1 inch cubes
1 lb stew beef, cut in 1 inch cubes
2 tablespoons butter
3–4 cups chicken stock
salt and pepper
$\frac{3}{4}$–1 can consommé
$\frac{1}{2}$ lb mushrooms, quartered
2 cup quantity rough puff or flaky pastry
1 egg, beaten to mix with $\frac{1}{2}$ teaspoon salt (for glaze)

Deep 9 inch pie dish

Method

Melt the butter in a heavy based casserole, and brown the venison on all sides over medium heat. Take out and brown the beef, also. Return venison to the pan with 3 cups of beef stock, cover and simmer on top of the stove for $1\frac{1}{2}$–2 hours or until the meat is very tender. Add more stock during cooking if the mixture gets dry. Taste for seasoning.

Make the pastry and chill 30 minutes. Set oven at hot (425°F).

Spread venison mixture in pie dish in layers with the mushrooms. Roll out dough to a circle, cut a strip to cover edge of pie dish, press it down well and brush with water. Lift the rest of dough onto a rolling pin and lay it carefully over the dish. Trim around the edge and seal the edges of dough with the back of a knife. This separates the layers so that the dough puffs up during cooking. Roll out dough trimmings and cut leaves for decoration. With the point of a knife make a hole in the center of the pie to allow steam to escape and arrange leaves around it.

Brush dough with beaten egg glaze and bake the pie in the heated oven for 20–25 minutes or until the pastry is puffed and brown. While the pie is still warm pour about 1 cup consommé through the hole in the center of the pie. Serve chilled.

Game, steak and mushroom pie is topped with rough puff pastry

Fillets of Venison Poivrade

2 lb boned loin of venison,
  or slices from top of haunch
3 tablespoons oil
$\frac{1}{4}$ cup port or red wine
black pepper, freshly ground
$\frac{1}{4}$ cup peanuts or cashews
$\frac{1}{3}$ cup raisins, soaked in
  hot water for 30 minutes
  and drained
2 tablespoons butter
6 slices of bread, cut into
  hearts and fried in a little
  hot olive oil and butter,
  mixed (for croûtes)

For sauce poivrade
$\frac{1}{2}$ cup chopped mushroom
  stems
$1\frac{1}{2}$ teaspoons tomato paste
2—3 tablespoons oil
1 small onion, diced
1 small carrot, diced
1 small stalk of celery, diced
1 tablespoon flour
$2\frac{1}{2}$ cups well-flavored stock
bouquet garni
$\frac{1}{2}$ cup red wine
2 tablespoons red wine vinegar
salt and pepper

Method
If using boned loin, cut venison into slices about $\frac{3}{4}$ inch thick. Lay them on a plate and sprinkle with 1 tablespoon oil, the port or red wine and plenty of freshly ground pepper. Cover and let stand for at least 1 hour.

To prepare sauce: heat the oil, add onion, carrot and celery and cook over low heat until they start to brown. Stir in the flour and continue cooking to a rich brown. Add two-thirds of the stock, the mushroom stems, tomato paste, bouquet garni and the wine. Bring mixture to a boil, stirring, reduce heat and simmer with the lid half-covering the pan for 20—25 minutes. Add half the remaining stock, bring to a boil again and skim. Now add

For venison poivrade, slice the meat before marinating in the oil and wine mixture

the remaining stock and repeat the process. Strain sauce, return it to the pan, add the vinegar and continue to simmer 6—7 minutes longer. Taste for seasoning and keep warm. Heat nuts and raisins in the butter and keep warm.

To cook steaks: heat a skillet or heavy frying pan, wipe pieces of venison with paper towels to remove moisture. Heat remaining oil and sauté them over high heat for about 4 minutes on each side. Arrange them on a warm platter with the heart-shaped croûtes between each steak, beginning and ending with a croûte. Reheat the sauce, stir in raisins and nuts and spoon some sauce into the center of the dish; serve the rest separately.

Venison Grenadins
(Steaks)

$1\frac{1}{2}$—2 lb boned loin of venison
thin slice of pork fat (for
  larding) – optional
2 tablespoons oil (for
  sautéing)
2 teaspoons juniper berries

For marinade
1 cup red wine
1 onion, sliced
1 carrot, sliced
large bouquet garni
6—8 peppercorns
2 tablespoons olive oil
2 teaspoons wine vinegar

For sauce
2 tablespoons oil
1 tablespoon finely diced onion
1 tablespoon finely diced carrot
$\frac{1}{2}$ stalk of celery, finely diced
1 tablespoon flour
2 cups beef stock
1 tablespoon red currant jelly
salt and pepper

Method
Tie venison in a neat roll, wrap in pork fat if you like, then cut across into 'grenadins' – steaks 1—1$\frac{1}{2}$ inches thick, similar to beef steak tournedos. Combine all ingredients for marinade and bring to a boil; cool. Pour marinade over the grenadins in a dish, cover and let stand for several hours or overnight in the refrigerator.

To prepare sauce: heat the oil and cook onion, carrot and celery until they begin to brown. Stir in flour and cook over low heat until very brown. Stir in the stock, bring to a boil, half-cover the pan and simmer 30—40 minutes. Skim well and strain, then return to the pan.

Strain marinade into the sauce and simmer 15—20 minutes, skimming occasion-

ally. Add red currant jelly, season to taste and simmer until the sauce is glossy and slightly thick.

Pat the grenadins dry with paper towels. Heat the oil and sauté the grenadins over fairly high heat for about 3 minutes on each side. After turning grenadins, sprinkle over the juniper berries with a little salt and pepper.

Transfer the grenadins to a warm platter, spoon over a little of the sauce and serve the rest separately. Hot chestnut croquettes are a good accompaniment.

Chestnut Croquettes

1 can (16 oz) unsweetened
  chestnut purée
2 shallots, chopped
1 tablespoon butter
salt and pepper
1 small egg, beaten to mix
deep fat (for frying)

For coating
$\frac{1}{4}$ cup seasoned flour (made
  with $\frac{1}{4}$ teaspoon salt and
  pinch of pepper)
1 egg, beaten to mix
$\frac{1}{2}$ cup dry white breadcrumbs

Method
Cook shallots in butter until soft but not brown. Mix them with the chestnut purée, season well and stir in the beaten egg. Shape the mixture into little balls the size of walnuts and coat with seasoned flour, egg and breadcrumbs. Place in a frying basket and fry in hot deep fat (375°F—385°F on a fat thermometer) until golden brown. Drain on paper towels.

Fillets of venison poivrade are arranged between heart-shaped croûtes; some of the sauce poivrade is spooned in the center

Wild rabbit in red wine is served with new potatoes tossed in butter and chopped parsley

Rabbit

The meat of the wild rabbit is not unlike chicken in flavor and texture but it has just enough gamy zest to make it fine eating. It is not good for roasting as it is too tough and dry. Rabbits that are sluggish and easy to shoot are usually sick and should not be eaten. Wild rabbits should be cooked until well done.

Wild Rabbit in Red Wine

1 wild rabbit, cut in serving pieces
1½ cups red wine
¼ cup seasoned flour (made with ¼ teaspoon salt and pinch of pepper)
¼ cup butter
12 baby onions, blanched and peeled
2–3 strips of lemon rind
few sprigs of parsley
2 stalks of celery, cut in pieces
1 bay leaf
kneaded butter (made with 1½ tablespoons butter and 2 teaspoons flour)
salt and pepper

For garnish
6–8 new potatoes, boiled and tossed in a little butter
1 tablespoon chopped parsley

Method
Toss rabbit in seasoned flour to coat. In a skillet, heat butter, add rabbit pieces and fry until well browned on all sides. Add onions and cook 2 minutes. Pour in the wine; tie lemon rind, parsley, celery and bay leaf in a cheesecloth bag and add to the skillet. Cover the pan tightly and simmer the meat for about 1 hour or until the rabbit is well done.

Transfer rabbit to a warm platter and discard the cheesecloth bag. Stir the kneaded butter into the liquid and bring to a boil, stirring constantly until the sauce thickens. Simmer 2 minutes and taste for seasoning. Spoon some of the sauce over the pieces of rabbit and serve remaining sauce separately.

Arrange a few new potatoes tossed in butter and chopped parsley around the dish and serve with cabbage stuffed with chestnuts.

Cabbage Stuffed with Chestnuts

1 firm head of green cabbage
1 lb chestnuts, skinned
1 onion, sliced
2 tablespoons butter
3 cups well-flavored stock
about ¾ cup brown sauce, or gravy (preferably from game)

Method
Set oven at moderate (350°F).

Trim the cabbage, removing outside leaves. Cook it in boiling salted water for 5 minutes, drain and refresh. Put chestnuts in a pan with the onion, butter and 2 cups of the stock. Cover and cook gently 25–30 minutes or until chestnuts are almost tender and the liquid has evaporated.

Cut a deep cross in the cabbage, curl back the outer leaves, cut out the center and fill with the chestnuts. Reshape the cabbage and fit it into a buttered casserole. Pour over remaining stock, cover and bake in heated oven for 45–50 minutes. Spoon over the brown sauce or gravy and return cabbage to the oven for 5–10 minutes longer.

Wild Rabbit with Lentils

2 small wild rabbits, cut in serving pieces
1 lb lentils
1–2 cloves of garlic, peeled
¼ cup flour
¼ cup butter
2 tablespoons olive oil
salt and pepper
2 medium onions, chopped
4 slices of bacon
1 cup (¼ lb) mushrooms, sliced

Method
Set oven at moderate (350°F). Soak the lentils according to package directions.

Cut garlic in half, rub rabbit pieces with cut sides and coat with flour. Heat 2 tablespoons butter with the oil and sauté rabbit until the pieces are well browned all over.

Drain the lentils, cover with fresh water, add 1 teaspoon salt and bring to a boil. Cover and simmer lentils for about 20 minutes. Drain and stir in the onions with remaining butter. Season to taste.

Rub a casserole with the cut sides of garlic and line the bottom with slices of bacon. Arrange a layer of lentils on the bacon, put the rabbit pieces on the lentils and cover with the remaining lentils. Sprinkle mushrooms over the top, cover tightly and bake in heated oven 1–1½ hours or until the rabbit is well done.

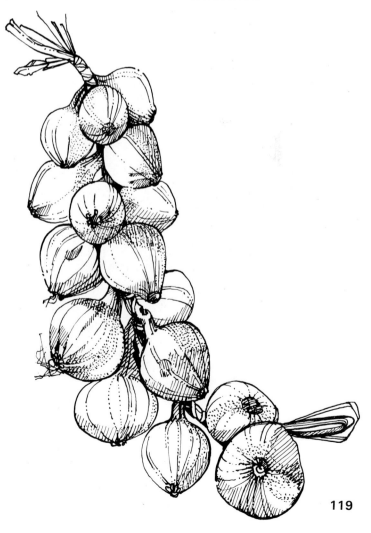

A tempting platter of formal hors d'oeuvre includes from left to right: Strasbourgeoise tartlets, choux puffs with cheese filling, tartlets Suisse, Fortnum and Mason frivolities, shrimp boats garnished with paprika, choux puffs, frivolities, salmon and cream cheese boats and triangular tartlets Jeanette

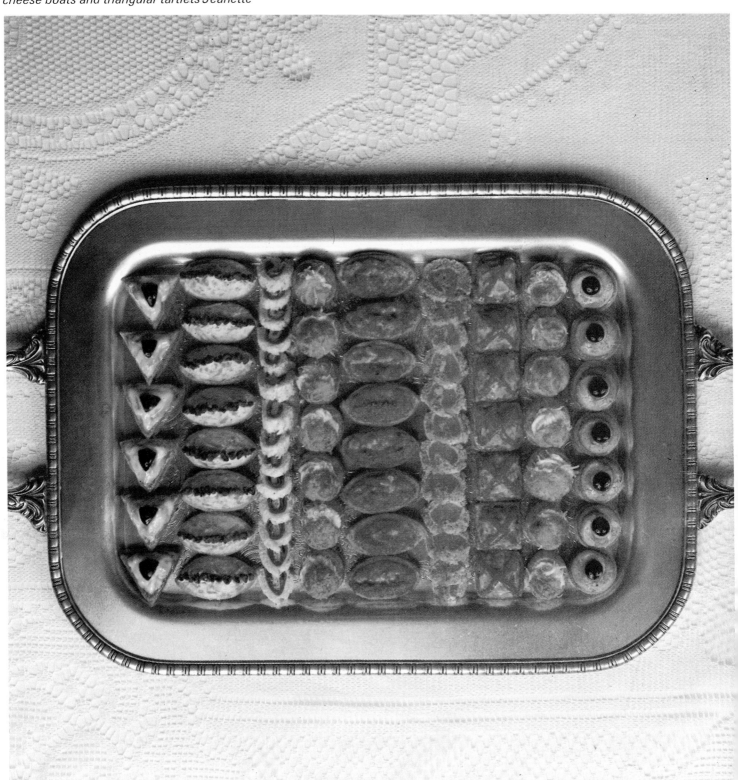

COCKTAIL PARTY HORS D'OEUVRE

Drinks are the foundation of a cocktail party but hors d'oeuvre add the elegance. To stand out against cocktails, hors d'oeuvre must have pronounced flavors — cheese, anchovy, chive or caviar — and the texture is equally important. Hot foods should be very hot, not tepid, and the cold ones that are so refreshing in summer should be thoroughly chilled. Avoid anything that wilts or dries out easily in the hot atmosphere of most parties; you'll find that many traditional canapés have a protective coating of aspic to keep them fresh. Try to vary the texture and color of the hors d'oeuvre as well as the flavor.

Don't tackle too many types of hors d'oeuvre at once; 8–10 different kinds should give enough variety for a group of 50 and 4–5 kinds are enough for parties of up to 24 people. The allowance made by most caterers for formal parties is 6 hors d'oeuvre or canapés per head, but people tend to eat more at informal parties, so make allowances for the audience.

Be sure to prepare well in advance making pastry, cutting up vegetables, combining mixtures, so they only need to be assembled and arranged on trays and platters before serving. Add eye appeal with plenty of parsley or watercress and colorful vegetables like tomatoes and lemons. Prepared trays of chilled foods can be kept fresh if they are covered with wax paper and damp paper towels or tucked down plastic wrap. Hors d'oeuvre for reheating can wait on baking sheets.

When platters are kept filled during the party, hors d'oeuvre will look as fresh at the end of the occasion as they did at the beginning. Other recipes for cocktail hors d'oeuvre were given in Volume 7.

Hors d'oeuvre for formal parties must be small enough to eat in one or two bites. Anything so small takes patience to prepare and each kind should be exactly the same size and have exactly the same decoration so its flavor can be easily identified. Tiny hors d'oeuvre look best arranged in rows or in geometric patterns on stainless steel or silver platters.

FORMAL HORS D'OEUVRE

PUFF PASTRIES

The following pastries freeze well; they can be shaped and frozen, then thawed and baked just before serving or they can be baked before freezing. If baked before freezing, they are best thawed, then reheated in a moderately low oven (325°F) for 8–10 minutes before serving.

Basic Recipe

2 cup quantity of puff pastry or puff pastry trimmings (see Volume 8) or 2 cup quantity of rough puff or flaky pastry (see Volume 5)
1 egg, beaten to mix with $\frac{1}{2}$ teaspoon salt (for glaze)
chosen filling (see right)

Method
Set the oven at hot (425°F).
Roll out the pastry dough to $\frac{1}{4}$ inch thickness, fill with chosen filling and shape as described. Transfer the pastries to a dampened baking sheet and chill 15 minutes. Bake in the heated oven for 8–12 minutes or until golden brown. Serve hot or transfer to a wire rack to cool.

Anchovy Fingers

Roll out the pastry dough to strips 6 inches wide and cut in half lengthwise, trimming the edges. Brush 1 rectangle with egg glaze and lay drained anchovy fillets crosswise on it at $1\frac{1}{2}$ inch intervals. Place the second rectangle on top and press down gently with a fingertip to outline the anchovies.

Brush with egg glaze and cut down between each fillet to form fingers. Decorate each finger in a lattice pattern with the back of a knife and bake as for basic recipe. Makes about 30 fingers.

Cheese Fingers

Roll out pastry dough to strips 6 inches wide and brush with egg glaze. Sprinkle generously with grated Parmesan cheese. Cut in half lengthwise, trim the edges and cut crosswise into rectangles 1 inch wide. Bake as for basic recipe. Makes about 80 fingers.

Chicken Liver Fingers

Melt 2 tablespoons butter in a frying pan and fry 1 chopped onion until soft. Add 1 cup chicken livers and sauté until brown on all sides but still pink in the center. Add 2 tablespoons brandy, a pinch of cayenne and plenty of seasoning and continue cooking 1 minute. Let cool, then chop the mixture finely.

Roll out pastry dough to a strip 6 inches wide and spoon the chicken liver mixture to one side of the center, but not to the edge. Brush the edge of the pastry with egg glaze, fold over one side to meet the other, covering the chicken liver mixture, and press the edges to seal. Trim the edges, brush with egg glaze and cut into 1-inch fingers. Bake as for basic recipe. Makes about 40 fingers.

Foie Gras Fingers

In the above recipe, replace the chicken liver mixture with canned pâté de foie gras, cut into sticks. Less expensive mousse of foie gras or liver pâté cannot be substituted as it melts during cooking.

Sausage Rolls

Roll out pastry dough to strips 6 inches wide, brush with egg glaze, and cut in half lengthwise, trimming the edges. Lay baby chipolata sausages along one edge of each strip and roll them up to enclose the sausages. Press gently to seal with the seam underneath and cut the roll between each sausage. Brush with egg glaze decorate with the back of a knife in a lattice pattern and bake as for basic recipe. Makes about 30 rolls.

Ham Crescents

Roll the pastry dough to a strip 6 inches wide, trim the edges, cut in half lengthwise, then crosswise to form 3 inch squares. Cut each square into 2 triangles.

Put a small teaspoon of finely chopped prosciutto, or finely chopped cooked ham mixed with a little Worcestershire sauce, in the center of each triangle. Roll up the dough, starting at the long edge, then roll on the table with your hand to elongate the roll slightly and seal it; shape it into a crescent. Brush crescents with egg glaze and bake as for basic recipe. Makes about 50 crescents.

Anchovy Diamonds

Roll the dough to a 10 X 20 inch rectangle. Trim the edges and cut it in half to form 2 squares. Spread 1 square with anchovy paste, set the other square on top and press lightly. Chill 15 minutes, brush with egg glaze, cut into $1\frac{1}{2}$ inch strips, then cut diagonally into diamonds. Bake as described. Makes about 40 diamonds.

Hot sausage rolls are one of many puff pastry cocktail hors d'oeuvre

To make Pastry Boats and Tartlet Shells

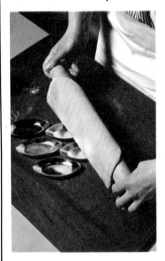

Lift dough on rolling pin and lay over molds

Work dough into molds with piece of floured dough

Cut dough off molds by rolling over with pin

TARTLETS

Tartlet cases of pie pastry can be filled with a wide variety of mixtures. The best size tartlet molds for cocktail hors d'oeuvre are round ones that are $1\frac{1}{4}$–$1\frac{3}{4}$ inches across, or boat shapes can be made in 2 inch long molds.

Baked tartlet or boat shells should not be filled more than 2 hours ahead as the pastry softens, but they can be baked ahead and stored in an airtight container for up to a week. The shells can also be frozen whether baked or unbaked.

Basic Recipe

$1\frac{1}{2}$ cup quantity of pie pastry or rich pie pastry dough (see Volume 1)
1 egg, beaten to mix with $\frac{1}{2}$ teaspoon salt (for glaze)
filling (see right)

This quantity makes about 20 tartlets or boats. Each of the following fillings fill 20 shells.

Method
Set oven at moderately hot (375°F).

Roll out pastry dough to just under $\frac{1}{4}$ inch thick. Arrange molds close together near the dough. Lift dough onto the rolling pin and lay it gently on top of the molds. Take a small piece of dough, dip it in flour and use it to work the dough down into each boat or tartlet mold. Roll the rolling pin over the tops of the molds to cut the pastry off the top of each one. Lift up each mold and pat the pastry down with your thumb dipped in flour.

Put a small piece of wax paper or foil, crumpled, and a few grains of rice in each mold; the paper and rice hold the pastry in position during baking. Put the molds on a baking sheet and bake blind in the heated oven for about 8 minutes or until the pastry is lightly browned. Remove paper and rice from shells, then continue baking 1–2 minutes. Leave pastry shells in the molds until they are nearly cold before removing them.

Tartlets Jeanette

1 cup finely chopped cooked chicken breasts
$\frac{1}{4}$ cup mayonnaise
few ripe olives, cut in pieces
1 cup aspic (see Volume 8)

Method
Mix the chicken with the mayonnaise and fill into the tartlet shells. Smooth tops, decorate with a piece of olive and coat with aspic on the point of setting.

Tartlets Suisse

$\frac{1}{2}$ cup finely diced cooked ham
$\frac{1}{2}$ cup finely diced Gruyère cheese
2–3 tablespoons mayonnaise
1 teaspoon Dijon-style mustard (or to taste)
$\frac{1}{2}$ slice of canned pimiento, drained and cut in thin strips
1 cup aspic (see Volume 8)

Method
Mix the ham and cheese with the mayonnaise and add mustard to taste. Fill the mixture into the tartlet shells. Smooth the tops, decorate with 2 strips of pimiento, crossed, and coat with aspic on the point of setting.

Strasbourgeoise

1 can (4 oz) mousse of foie gras
small can truffles
2–3 tablespoons heavy cream
1 cup aspic (see Volume 8)

Pastry bag and $\frac{3}{8}$ inch plain tube

Method
Drain the truffles, reserving the liquid, and slice them thinly. Beat the truffle liquid into the foie gras with enough cream so the mixture is soft

enough to pipe. Put the mixture into a pastry bag fitted with a $\frac{3}{8}$ inch plain tube and fill the tartlet shells. Top each tartlet with a slice of truffle and coat with aspic on the point of setting.

Shrimp Boats

$1\frac{1}{2}$ cups finely chopped cooked
   shrimps
$\frac{1}{3}$ cup mayonnaise
1 tablespoon tomato paste
   (or to taste)
paprika (for sprinkling)

Method
Mix the shrimps with the mayonnaise and tomato paste to taste. Fill the mixture into the boat shells, mounding it to a peak along the center. Sprinkle one side of the boat generously with paprika.

Smoked Salmon Boats

$\frac{1}{4}$ lb smoked salmon, finely
   chopped
1 package (3 oz) cream cheese
4–6 tablespoons heavy cream
black pepper, freshly ground
2 tablespoons capers, drained
   and coarsely chopped

Method
Beat the cream cheese with enough cream to soften it. Add the smoked salmon with more cream, if necessary, to make a soft mixture and season well with black pepper. Fill into boat shells, mounding the mixture to a peak along the center and sprinkle the peak with chopped capers.

FRIVOLITIES

Frivolities take less time than the traditional pastry or bread-based canapés. They are made with slices of bread spread with filling that are rolled and chilled so they can be cut in slices to show their spiral of filling.

   The rolls can be prepared a day ahead or they can be frozen. Slice them not more than 2 hours before serving so they do not dry out.

Basic Recipe

If possible use unsliced bread as it can be spread easily with butter and sliced more thinly than ready sliced bread.

   Spread the cut end of the loaf with softened butter or mayonnaise (according to the individual recipe), slice the bread about $\frac{1}{4}$ inch thick and trim the crusts. Add the filling, roll and wrap as tightly as possible in foil. Chill at least 4 hours or until firm. With a sharp knife, cut the roll in $\frac{1}{2}$ inch slices to serve.

Beau Monsieur

Work Gorgonzola or Roquefort cheese through a sieve and beat in enough softened butter to make a paste. Spread on wholewheat bread and roll.

Délicieuse

Spread white bread with butter, add a slice of prosciutto and roll.

Russe

Spread rye bread with cream cheese, softened with a little cream. Sprinkle with finely chopped scallions, finely chopped dill pickles and seasoning, and roll.

Fortnum and Mason

Fortnum and Mason is one of the most famous grocery stores in England.

   Spread wholewheat bread with butter, top with very thinly sliced smoked salmon, sprinkle with black pepper and a little lemon juice and roll.

BOUCHEES AND CHOUX PUFFS

Miniature choux puffs and bouchées of puff pastry about $1\frac{1}{4}$ inches in diameter are great favorites as hors d'oeuvres. Bouchée cases can be made ahead and kept in an airtight container or frozen (for instructions, see Volume 8), but choux puffs tend to harden if they are baked more than 6–8 hours in advance.

   Both bouchées and puffs should be split and filled, using a demitasse spoon, not more than 2 hours ahead. If they are to be served hot, heat them in a moderately low oven (325°F) for 10–15 minutes or until very hot.

   Any of the following mixtures are enough to fill choux puffs made with a 3–4 egg quantity of dough or bouchées made with a 2 cup quantity of puff pastry – about 30 hors d'oeuvre.

Smoked Oysters à l'Indienne

1 can ($3\frac{1}{2}$ oz) smoked oysters,
   drained and chopped
1 teaspoon butter
1 teaspoon curry powder
1 cup white sauce

Method
In a small saucepan melt the butter, add the curry powder and cook gently, stirring, for 1 minute. Stir in the white sauce and chopped oysters. Serve hot.

Sultane

$\frac{3}{4}$ cup finely chopped cooked
   chicken breast
$\frac{3}{4}$ cup velouté sauce
$\frac{1}{4}$ cup shelled pistachios,
   blanched and halved
salt and pepper

Method
Mix the chopped chicken, velouté sauce and pistachios and season well. Serve hot.

Lobster à l'Hongroise

$\frac{3}{4}$ cup finely chopped lobster
   meat
$1\frac{1}{2}$ teaspoons butter
$1\frac{1}{2}$ teaspoons paprika
1 teaspoon tomato paste
$\frac{3}{4}$ cup béchamel sauce

Method
In a small saucepan melt the butter, add the paprika and cook gently for 2 minutes. Stir in the tomato paste, then the béchamel sauce and mix well. Add the lobster meat and taste for seasoning. Serve hot.

Salmon and caviar checkerboard makes a spectacular hors d'oeuvre

Fillings continued

Eggs with Olives

2 hard-cooked eggs, finely
   chopped
½ cup ripe Italian-style
   olives, pitted and chopped
about ½ cup tomato sauce

Method
Combine the eggs and olives
with enough tomato sauce to
bind the mixture. Serve hot or
cold.

Cheese with Butter

½ cup white sauce, made with
   1 tablespoon butter,
   1 tablespoon flour and
   ½ cup milk
½ cup finely grated Parmesan
   cheese
¼ cup finely grated Gruyère
   cheese
½ teaspoon Dijon-style mustard
salt and pepper
½ cup butter, softened
2 tablespoons grated Parmesan
   cheese (for sprinkling) –
   optional

*Pastry bag and ⅜ inch plain tube
(optional)*

Method
Make the white sauce, let cool
slightly, then beat in the
cheese, mustard and plenty of
seasoning. When cool, beat in
the butter and taste for
seasoning. If you like, fill the
mixture into choux puffs or
bouchées with a pastry bag
and ⅜ inch plain tube. Serve
cold.
   For choux puffs, sprinkle
with grated Parmesan cheese
and replace lid at a slant.

CHECKERBOARD

An effective checkerboard can
be made with any ingredients
of contrasting color. The
board can be assembled up to
4 hours ahead and kept,
tightly covered with plastic
wrap, in a cool place.

Salmon and Caviar Checkerboard

½ lb smoked salmon
1 jar (4 oz) caviar
1 package (3 oz) cream cheese
2–3 tablespoons heavy cream
10 slices of wholewheat bread
black pepper, freshly ground
10 slices of white bread
¼ cup butter, creamed
juice of 1 lemon
bunch of parsley (for garnish)

For a special occasion, use
imported sturgeon caviar and
Scottish smoked salmon for
the checkerboard. However,
it looks just as effective made
with domestic smoked salmon
and lumpfish caviar.

Method
Beat the cream cheese with
enough cream to make a soft
mixture and spread it on the
wholewheat bread slices.
Sprinkle with black pepper
and top each slice with
salmon. Trim the crusts and
cut each slice in 4 squares.
   Spread the white bread
slices with creamed butter and
spread with caviar. Sprinkle
with lemon juice, trim the
crusts and cut each slice in
4 squares.
   Arrange the salmon and
caviar squares alternately in a
checkerboard pattern on a
large platter and surround the
edge with parsley sprigs.

Other Checkerboard Suggestions

1 Set sliced cooked ham or
tongue on brown bread spread
with sour cream flavored with
Dijon-style mustard to contrast with chopped hard-
cooked egg mixed with mayonnaise and chopped chives
spread on white bread.
2 Set sliced cooked chicken
breast on white bread spread
with mayonnaise flavored with
finely chopped sweet pickles
to contrast with rye bread
spread with softened cream
cheese, sprinkled with black
pepper and topped with a
cucumber slice. Top each
cucumber slice with half a
cherry tomato, fixed to the
cucumber with a little cream
cheese.

CROQUETTES AND BEIGNETS

Any of the croquettes and
savory beignets given in the
Cooking Course make good
hors d'oeuvre.
   Shape croquettes in 1½ inch
cork shapes or in 1 inch balls
and coat them with egg and
breadcrumbs. They can be
kept covered in the refrigerator for up to 24 hours.
   Choux pastry dough for
beignets can be made up to
24 hours ahead and kept
covered in the refrigerator.
   Both beignets and croquettes should be deep fried and
served within 10 minutes. If
you like, pass a dip such as
herb tomato sauce or devil
sauce (see Volume 7) separately.

Aigrettes

2 egg whites
about ⅔ cup grated Parmesan
   cheese
black pepper, freshly ground
deep fat (for frying)

Makes 24 aigrettes.

Method
Beat the egg whites until
broken up and stir in enough
grated Parmesan cheese to
make a mixture that just drops
from a spoon. Season highly
with pepper.
   Heat the deep fat to 375°F
on a fat thermometer and
gently drop teaspoons of the
mixture into the hot deep fat.
Fry a few spoonsful at a time
until puffed and brown, drain
thoroughly on paper towels
and serve beignets at once.

Herb Tomato Sauce

3–4 tomatoes, peeled, seeded
   and chopped or 1 can (16 oz)
   canned tomatoes, crushed
2 tablespoons oil
1 clove of garlic, crushed
1 teaspoon oregano
1 teaspoon thyme
bay leaf
salt and pepper

Makes ¾ cup sauce.

Method
Heat the oil, add the tomatoes, garlic, herbs and seasoning and cook, stirring, for
about 15 minutes or until the
tomatoes are pulpy. Discard
the bay leaf, work the mixture
through a sieve or purée it in a
blender and taste for seasoning.

ASSORTED CANAPES

Traditional canapés are based on rounds or fingers of bread or toast that are topped with colorful combinations of ingredients often decorated with piped curlicues of mayonnaise. They can be made 5–6 hours ahead if they are tightly covered with plastic wrap or with wax paper topped with a damp cloth and kept in the refrigerator or a cool place.

Mushroom Canapés

1 cup mushrooms, finely chopped
1 tablespoon butter
1 shallot or scallion, finely chopped
2 teaspoons chopped parsley
salt
black pepper, freshly ground
12 rounds (1½ inches each) white bread, fried in
2 tablespoons oil and
2 tablespoons butter and drained (for croûtes)
2 tablespoons grated Parmesan cheese

Makes 12 canapés.

Method
Heat the butter and fry the shallot or scallion over low heat until soft but not browned. Add the mushrooms and cook over medium heat until all the moisture has evaporated. Add the parsley and season to taste.
Spread the mixture on the croûtes and sprinkle with grated cheese. Just before serving, broil until browned. Serve hot.

Clam and Spinach Canapés

1 can (7½ oz) minced clams, drained
1 package frozen spinach, cooked and drained
2 tablespoons butter
2 tablespoons grated Parmesan cheese
12 slices white bread, toasted

1½ inch plain cookie cutter

Makes 24 canapés.

Method
Cut 24 rounds (1½ inches each) from the toasted bread. Work the spinach in a blender until puréed.
Heat the butter, add the spinach and cook, stirring until dry. Take from the heat, add the minced clams and spread the mixture on the toast rounds not more than 3 hours before serving. Sprinkle with grated cheese. Just before serving, broil until browned and serve hot.

Onion and Tomato Canapés

1 large Bermuda or other mild onion, finely chopped
¼ cup tomato paste
2 tablespoons butter
2 teaspoons basil
salt
black pepper, freshly ground
pinch of sugar
12 rounds (1½ inches each) white bread, fried in
2 tablespoons oil and
2 tablespoons butter and drained (for croûtes)

Makes 12 canapés.

Method
Heat the butter and fry the onion until soft but not browned. Take from the heat, add the tomato paste, basil, seasoning and sugar to taste. Spread the mixture on the croûtes. A short time before serving, reheat in a moderate oven (350°F) for 8–10 minutes and serve hot.

Egg and Anchovy Canapés

Spread 1½ inch rounds of plain or toasted white bread with mayonnaise. Cover one side with sieved hard-cooked egg yolk and the other side with finely chopped hard-cooked egg white and press down lightly. Lay a fillet of anchovy across the middle. Serve cold.

Smoked Salmon Canapés

Cut rounds of buttered wholewheat bread and very thinly sliced smoked salmon with a 1½ inch cookie cutter. Set salmon on the bread and, using a paper decorating cone, decorate with a curlicue of green mayonnaise. Serve cold.

Caviar Canapés

Spread caviar on buttered 1½ inch circles of plain or toasted white bread. Top with paper thin slices of lemon. Serve cold.

Tomato and Egg Canapés

Cut 1½ inch rounds of plain or toasted buttered wholewheat bread and top with thin slices of hard-cooked egg, the same size as the bread. Decorate with peeled cherry tomato halves. Serve cold.

Ham or Salami Canapés

Cut 1½ inch rounds of buttered rye bread and spread thinly with Dijon-style mustard. Top with 1½ inch rounds of thinly sliced ham or salami and, using a paper decorating cone, decorate with spirals of mayonnaise. Set a piece of ripe olive in the center of each spiral. Serve cold.

An attractive presentation of assorted canapés includes from left to right: egg and anchovy, salami with olive, smoked salmon, caviar topped with lemon, and egg and tomato

INFORMAL HORS D'OEUVRE

Food for informal parties should be as simple as possible with little last-minute preparation and no serving problems. Avoid elaborate canapés and look for ideas like miniature kebabs, fondue and the Italian garlic and anchovy dip called bagna cauda that are fun to serve and delicious to eat. All are easy to make ahead and your friends will be happy to serve themselves while enjoying the party.

STUFFED MUSHROOMS

Mushrooms can be stuffed with a variety of mixtures and they make delicious appetizers as well as hors d'oeuvre. Serve them on toothpicks or, for more formal occasions, set the mushrooms on a round of toast.

Mushrooms with Snails

4 cups (1 lb) medium button mushrooms
24 canned snails, drained

For garlic butter
2–3 cloves of garlic, crushed
$\frac{1}{2}$ cup butter
2 shallots or scallions, finely chopped
1 tablespoon chopped parsley
squeeze of lemon juice
salt and pepper

Makes 25–30 stuffed mushrooms.

Method
To make garlic butter: heat 2 tablespoons butter and fry the shallot or scallion until soft but not browned. Let cool. Cream the remaining butter and beat in the shallot, garlic, parsley, lemon juice and plenty of seasoning.

Discard the stems from the mushroom caps and set a snail in the center of each one. Top with a teaspoon of garlic butter and set on a buttered baking sheet.

A short time before serving, bake in a moderate oven (350°F) for 10–12 minutes or until the mushrooms are tender.

Stuffed Mushrooms with Ham

4 cups (1 lb) medium button mushrooms
$\frac{1}{4}$ cup finely chopped cooked ham
$\frac{1}{4}$ cup butter
1 shallot or scallion, finely chopped
1 clove of garlic, crushed (optional)
$\frac{1}{2}$ cup fresh white breadcrumbs
2 tablespoons chopped parsley
salt and pepper

Makes about 25–30 stuffed mushrooms.

Method
Remove mushroom stems from caps and chop stems. In a skillet melt 2 tablespoons butter, add shallot or scallion and cook until soft but not browned. Add chopped mushroom stems with the garlic, if used, and cook until soft. Add remaining butter, heat until melted, then stir in the ham, breadcrumbs, chopped parsley and seasoning.

Fill the mixture into the mushroom caps and set them on a buttered baking sheet. A short time before serving, bake in a moderate oven (350°F) for 10–12 minutes or until mushrooms are tender, or brown them under the broiler.

GREEK PASTRY FINGERS

Greek phyllo pastry is available in many specialty food stores, and like puff pastry, it can be filled with a wide variety of savory mixtures. The pastries can be shaped, then frozen to bake later.

Basic Recipe

1 lb package phyllo pastry dough
$\frac{1}{3}$ cup melted butter (for brushing)
chosen filling (see right)

Each of the fillings is enough for this quantity of pastry and makes about 40 fingers.

Method
Set the oven at hot (400°F) and butter a baking sheet.

Spread 1 sheet phyllo on a board, brush with melted butter and cover with another sheet. Brush half this sheet with butter and fold the sheets in two so one half is on top of the other.

Spoon the filling along the folded edge, leaving 1 inch of space at each end and a 2 inch gap in the middle of the filling. Roll up the sheet in a cylinder to enclose the filling and cut the roll in half.

Set the rolls on the prepared baking sheet and shape the remaining pastry in the same way.

Watchpoint: keep the unused sheets of pastry covered with a damp cloth while working, as they dry and disintegrate quickly.

Brush the fingers with butter and bake them in the heated oven for 15–20 minutes or until golden brown. Serve hot or cold.

Chili Filling

1–2 hot green chilies (or to taste)
1 lb ground beef
2 tablespoons oil
1 onion, chopped
2 cups stock
1 clove of garlic, crushed
$\frac{1}{2}$ teaspoon ground cumin
1 teaspoon paprika
$\frac{1}{2}$ teaspoon oregano
salt
paprika (for sprinkling)

Method
Hold the chili over a flame with a fork to char the skin, then peel it, cut in half and discard the core and seeds; chop it finely.

Watchpoint: handle chili with rubber gloves as chili oils can burn the skin.

In a saucepan heat the oil and fry the onion until soft. Add the beef and cook over medium heat until browned. Add the stock, garlic, chopped chili, cumin, paprika, oregano and salt, cover and simmer 1 hour, stirring occasionally. The mixture should be -thick and rich. If thin, remove the lid and continue cooking until the moisture evaporates; taste for seasoning. Sprinkle the fingers with paprika before baking.

Cocktail party hors d'oeuvre

Cheese and Almond Filling

½ lb feta cheese, crumbled
1 cup slivered almonds, browned and chopped
1 egg, beaten to mix
black pepper, freshly ground

Method
Beat the cheese with the egg until smooth. Stir in the almonds and add pepper to taste.

Seafood Filling

1 cup (½ lb) cooked chopped shrimps, lobster meat or crab meat
2 eggs, beaten to mix
½ teaspoon anchovy paste
pinch of dry mustard
pinch of cayenne
dash of Worcestershire sauce

Method
Mix the seafood with the eggs and add the seasonings to taste — the mixture should be spicy.

Melting Greek pastry fingers with chili filling are sprinkled with paprika before baking

Bagna cauda — leave your guests to help themselves to crisp vegetables and salad for dipping in the garlic and anchovy flavored dip

FONDUES AND DIPS

For informal parties, fondues and dips are ideal as they require little preparation and guests can choose their favorite crackers or vegetables for dipping.

Fondue au Champagne

2–2½ cups (¾ lb) grated
  Emmenthal cheese
2–2½ cups (¾ lb) grated
  Gruyère cheese
1 cup Champagne
1 tablespoon flour
2 tablespoons brandy
1 can truffle pieces (optional)
black pepper, freshly ground
French bread, cut in cubes
  (for dipping)

Makes about 4 cups fondue.

Method
Toss the cheese in the flour. Put the cheeses in a heavy-based pan with the Champagne and bring to a boil over moderate heat, stirring constantly in a figure of eight pattern.
Watchpoint: the fondue will separate if stirred too fast or heated too quickly but, at the same time, you must be careful not to cook it too slowly or it will separate when the cheese melts.
  Add the brandy, truffle pieces and truffle liquor, if used, and season with plenty of pepper. Bring the mixture just back to a boil – it should be creamy in consistency. Keep it warm over a table burner and serve cubes of French bread with long fondue forks for dipping.

The original **fondue** (meaning melted) was made of eggs and grated cheese, but many others have been invented in the last few years and the term now has the more general meaning of a hot mixture for dipping.
  Recipes for Swiss cheese fondue and fondue Brillat-Savarin were given in Volume 15 and a recipe for fondue Bourguignonne was given in Volume 5.

Bagna Cauda

2 cans (2 oz each) anchovy
  fillets, chopped
4–6 cloves of garlic, crushed
1 cup olive oil

For dipping
celery sticks
carrot sticks
zucchini sticks
radishes
green onions
Belgian endive, divided into
  leaves
green pepper strips

Makes about 1½ cups dip.

Method
Soak the vegetables in ice water for 1 hour before serving; drain thoroughly on paper towels and arrange on a platter or in a deep bowl.
  In a mortar and pestle or in a blender work the garlic and anchovy with a little olive oil until smooth.
  Stir in the remaining oil and heat gently for 10 minutes; do not let the mixture boil. Set over a table burner and serve chilled vegetables for dipping separately

Fritto Misto

Select four from the following suggestions.

1 small eggplant, sliced
2 zucchini, sliced
½ small cauliflower, divided
  into sprigs
1 cup (¼ lb) mushrooms,
  stems trimmed level with
  caps
bunch of scallions, trimmed
  3 inches long
1 green pepper, cored, seeded
  and cut in strips
10–12 green beans, trimmed
10–12 medium shrimps
deep fat (for frying)

For batter
¼ cup flour
pinch of salt
2 egg yolks
1 tablespoon melted butter
  or oil
½ cup milk
1 egg white

For dip
3 tablespoons chopped fresh
  basil or dill
1 cup plain yogurt

Quantities of batter and dip are enough for 4 of the suggested ingredients, so choose your favorites from the list above. Serves 6–8 people for hors d'oeuvre.

Method
To make the dip: stir the herb into the yogurt, spoon into a bowl and chill well.
  To make the batter: sift flour with salt into a bowl, make a well in the center and add egg yolks and melted butter or oil. Add milk gradually, mixing to form a smooth batter, and beat thoroughly. Stand in a cool place (not the refrigerator) for 30 minutes or until ready to use. Prepare the ingredients for frying.
  A short time before serving, heat the deep fat to 375°F on a fat thermometer. Whip egg white until it holds a stiff peak and fold into the batter. Dip the ingredients into the batter, drain slightly and lower into the hot fat. Fry them, a few at a time, until golden brown and drain on paper towels. Keep them warm in a moderate oven (350°F) with the door open. Serve at once with the chilled yogurt dip.

Crab Meat Dip

2 cups (1 lb) crab meat
1 can (8 oz) water chestnuts,
  drained and chopped
2 tablespoons soy sauce
½ cup mayonnaise
1 tablespoon chopped fresh
  ginger root
6–8 crab claws for garnish –
  optional (for dipping)
bread sticks (for serving)
celery sticks (for serving)

This recipe was first given in Volume 15.

Method
Combine all the ingredients, pile in a bowl and chill. Garnish with crab claws, if you like, and serve bread sticks and celery sticks for dipping.

Fritto misto is served with yogurt dip (recipe is on page 133)

MINIATURE KEBABS

Miniature kebabs are good for an outdoor party, where guests can do their own cooking on a barbecue or miniature Hibachi. You can leave ingredients and skewers ready for guests to make their own combinations or have the kebabs prepared for broiling.

For indoor parties, the kebabs should be broiled in the kitchen (unless the room is well ventilated).

These recipes serve 6–8 people for hors d'oeuvre or 3 as a main course.

Shrimp Kebabs

Marinate 1 lb medium peeled, uncooked shrimps in 2 tablespoons oil, juice of 1 lemon and 1 crushed clove of garlic (optional) for 1–2 hours. Thread on skewers and sprinkle lightly with paprika before broiling.

Lamb Kebabs

Cut 1 lb lean shoulder of lamb in ½-inch cubes and marinate in a mixture of 2 tablespoons oil, ¼ cup red wine, 1 teaspoon thyme, 1 bay leaf and freshly ground black pepper for up to 8 hours. Drain and thread on skewers for broiling.

Anticuchos

Cut 1 lb beef sirloin or fillet steak into ½ inch cubes. Discard stem and seeds from 1 fresh hot green chili and chop it, using rubber gloves to protect you skin from the chili oils.

Mix 2 tablespoons oil, 2 tablespoons red wine vinegar, pinch of salt, pinch of freshly ground black pepper, 1 crushed clove of garlic, ¼ teaspoon oregano, ¼ teaspoon ground cumin and ¼ teaspoon paprika, add the beef and let marinate 12–24 hours. Drain beef, thread on skewers and brush with marinade during broiling.

COCKTAIL SANDWICH LOAVES

Tiny cocktail sandwiches tend to dry out, but they keep fresh and look attractive if they are made from a hollowed crusty loaf of bread, then piled back into the crust for serving.

Basic Recipe

Cut the top off a round 2 lb crusty loaf. Holding the knife vertically, cut around the sides, but not through the bottom, to detach the crusty sides from the center. Holding the knife horizontally, insert it at the base of the loaf and cut to right and left, not quite through the sides of the loaf, so the center of the loaf can be removed. Lift it out and slice it in the thinnest possible rounds, spreading every other round with filling before slicing.

Put the rounds together to make sandwiches, cut them in four and replace in the loaf. Add the lid and wrap tightly until serving. The same method can be followed for a rectangular bread loaf.

Roquefort Spread

$\frac{1}{2}$ lb Roquefort cheese
$\frac{1}{2}$ lb cream cheese
2 tablespoons cognac
about $\frac{1}{4}$ cup heavy cream

Method
Work the Roquefort and cream cheeses through a sieve and beat in the cognac with enough cream to make a soft mixture. Spread on white or wholewheat bread.

Tongue Spread

$\frac{1}{2}$ lb cooked tongue, finely chopped
$\frac{1}{2}$ cup sour cream
1 teaspoon Dijon-style mustard
1 scallion, finely chopped

Method
Beat all the ingredients until thoroughly combined. Spread on rye bread.

Ham Spread

$\frac{1}{2}$ lb cooked lean ham, finely chopped
$\frac{1}{4}$ cup butter, softened
2 tablespoons Madeira
salt and pepper (optional)

Method
Cream the butter, gradually beat in the ham, followed by the Madeira; taste for seasoning. Spread on wholewheat bread.

Tuna and Walnut Spread

1 can (7 oz) tuna in oil, drained and flaked
$\frac{1}{3}$ cup walnut pieces, chopped
$\frac{1}{2}$ cup mayonnaise
salt
black pepper, freshly ground

Method
Pound the tuna in a mortar and pestle and stir in the mayonnaise or work it in a blender with the mayonnaise until smooth. Stir in the walnuts, season to taste and spread on white bread.

CHEESE BALLS

Many cheese mixtures that are excellent with cocktails have become classics, such as Cheddar cheese and port or cream cheese and chives. The mixture can be rolled into walnut-sized balls and speared on toothpicks, or it can be shaped into 1 large ball for spreading on crackers. Chill cheese balls thoroughly before serving.

Cheddar Cheese with Port

Cream $\frac{1}{3}$ cup butter and gradually beat in $1\frac{1}{2}$ cups (6 oz) grated Cheddar cheese with $\frac{1}{4}$ cup port. Shape the mixture into balls and coat with $\frac{1}{2}$ cup finely chopped pecans or walnuts.

Cream Cheese and Chives

Beat 1 cup (8 oz) cream cheese until smooth and work in $\frac{1}{2}$ cup sour cream, $\frac{1}{4}$ cup chopped chives, salt, freshly ground black pepper to taste and 1 clove of garlic, crushed, if you like. Stir in $\frac{1}{2}$ cup bread-crumbs made from dry white bread. Shape balls and coat with $\frac{1}{2}$ cup browned bread-crumbs.

MINIATURE MEATBALLS

Meatballs add pleasant variety to a cocktail party. They can be made ahead and kept warm in a chafing dish or put on toothpicks. A popular recipe is Swedish Köttbullar.

Köttbullar (Swedish Meatballs)

$\frac{1}{2}$ lb ground beef
$\frac{1}{4}$ lb ground pork
$\frac{1}{4}$ lb ground veal
$\frac{1}{2}$ cup fresh white breadcrumbs
$1\frac{1}{2}$ cups milk
$\frac{1}{2}$ onion, finely chopped
$\frac{1}{4}$ cup butter
1 egg
salt and pepper
1 tablespoon flour
1 cup heavy cream

Makes 18–20 meatballs.

Method
Soak the breadcrumbs in the milk. Fry the onion in 1 table-spoon of the butter until soft but not browned.

In a bowl mix the beef, pork, veal, onion, egg, and bread mixture with plenty of salt and pepper and beat with a wooden spoon until the mixture comes away from the sides of the bowl; shape into walnut-sized balls.

In a chafing dish or skillet, melt the remaining butter and fry the meatballs, a few at a time, over medium heat until evenly browned on all sides. Take out, add the flour and cook, stirring, until browned.

Add the cream and bring the sauce to a boil, stirring. Taste for seasoning, replace the meatballs, cover the pan and cook over low heat for 10 minutes. Keep warm in a chafing dish or over a table burner or serve on individual toothpicks.

INDEX
(Volume 17)

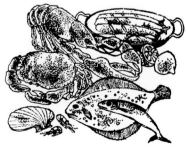

NOTES